MARJORIE REED'S PARTY BOOK

Entertaining with More Style than Money

By
Marjorie Reed
with Kalia Lulow

illustrated by Robert Penny

Ballantine Books·New York

Published in the United States
by Ballantine Books, a division
of Random House, Inc., New
York, and simultaneously in
Canada by Random House of
Canada Limited, Toronto,
Canada.

Library of Congress Catalog
Card Number: 81-066666
ISBN 0-345-29609-5
Designed by Michaelis/Carpelis
Design Assoc. Inc.

Front cover photograph by
Anthony Loew
Back cover photograph of
Marjorie Reed by Donald Piper
Calligraphy by Denis Paul Lund
Silhouette art by Heather Taylor

Manufactured in the United
States of America
First Ballantine Books Edition:
October 1981

10 9 8 7 6 5 4 3 2 1

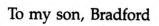

To my son, Bradford

Special thanks to my
mother Anne L. Kahn, and
Parker Ladd and Dr. Murray
Jonas, for their support
and friendship—and to
my friends, without whom
there would be no parties.

Marjorie Reed

Acknowledgments

We would like to thank
our cooking consultant,
Marilyn Kelly, for her
guidance and
supervision. Ms. Kelly is
a gourmet cooking
instructor and lecturer in
her home town of
Huntington, West
Virginia, and throughout
the Southeast. Her
expertise comes from a
solid background. She
studied at
Lavarenne École de Cuisine
in Paris.
She couples this with a
native ability to make the
complexities of cooking
understandable and fun.

Our overqualified, and
consequently terrific,
typist, Arri Parker, also
deserves a round of
applause.

And lastly, continuing
thanks to Joelle
Delbourgo, our editor,
whose enthusiasm and
skill made the whole
process a pleasure.

Marjorie Reed
Kalia Lulow

Table of Contents

MARJORIE REED'S PARTY BOOK

CHAPTER •1•

THROW A PARTY... DON'T LET IT THROW YOU!

The prospect of throwing a party should light up your life, animate your spirits, stimulate your imagination and, yes, even make you smile.

A party brings people together to share good feelings and good times. It is a gift of love, a demonstration that you care enough to give of your time and energy to others. A party is for anyone who ever had a friend or ever wanted to make a new one.

But be honest. When you think about throwing a party, what goes through your mind?

"Oh, I'll have to change how the house looks! Get new dishes. Learn to cook new foods. Spend time and money I don't have. Represent myself as something more than I usually am. Adopt a role—'Superhost.'"

Good heavens! No wonder you get nervous when you think about throwing a party. It's no gift of yourself to your friends. It's major surgery! You try to mold yourself into what you think a host *should* be.

It's enough work just to get the food ready and the house clean without putting yourself through the wringer.

HOW CAN YOU ENTERTAIN WITH MORE STYLE THAN MONEY?

Even the most anxious host can imagine throwing a successful party with an unlimited budget. That's easy. You just pay a lot to have other people take care of everything for you. But is that the kind of party you really want to give?

There is another way! No matter how busy your schedule, cramped your home, or tight your budget, you *can* learn to entertain with ease and style. All you have to do is throw out a few worn-out rules:

You don't have to be a gourmet cook to throw a dinner party. Simple food, prepared carefully and presented beautifully, is the best idea.

You don't have to own a palatial home to have a group of people over. With a dose of cleverness, even a studio apartment can be made spacious.

You don't have to have a lot of furniture. No table—but able; no chair—sit anywhere! That's the spirit.

You don't have to spend a lot of money on decorations to make a room look stunning. Mother Nature provides a myriad of beautiful resources you can bring indoors—rocks, shells, flowers and wild reeds, vegetables and fruit from the local market. The list is endless!

You don't have to impress people with what you have. It's how you do things that counts.

A party should be a natural extension of your own personality and life style. It should reflect what you like best about yourself. Its grandeur should be the result of the best of your abilities and imagination.

The point of entertaining is *not* to outspend, outdecorate, or outcook the "competition." It is to communicate your own inherent sense of life, of caring, of comfort. So discard those old-fashioned, pressure-filled attitudes. Free yourself, and you'll see your entertaining skills blossom. Concentrate on your strengths.

You do have just what's needed to throw a successful party! Yourself! A successful party is not made by the softness of upholstery or the expense of hors d'oeuvres. It is made by sharing and caring with friends in a spirit of open affection and fun. (Just think about the ghastly stiff parties you've been to where the food and decor were grand but the company and

spirit were boring. No amount of window dressing can make a successful party.

You do have natural talents and style on which to build your entertaining skills. Each of us possesses unconscious skills. Our personal taste and style are acted out in a thousand little ways every day. When you learn to identify your abilities, you build a style that is the result of confidence, not of insecurity.

You do have imagination, and imagination is free! No matter what your environment, you can transform it into a festive party setting through cleverness and imagination.

Any situation can be a party: an intimate dinner for two lovers; a shared conversation between two good friends; a carefully planned dinner party for twelve; a houseful of milling guests mixing and meeting new acquaintances. A party is even one person alone with a beautiful dinner tray set up with a special concern for comfort and taste. It is a vehicle for letting the emotions of care, love, and joy find expression.

The Steps to Successful Entertaining

All my life I have found pleasure and joy from bringing people together in special party environments. This is why I want to share my efforts with you. This is neither a book of etiquette nor a cookbook. It is a handbook that you can use over and over again—a guide for developing your own entertaining style.

Each chapter is a road map to self-discovery. The Party Questionnaire in Chapter 3 will help you identify your inherent entertaining strengths, preferences, and potential. "New Uses for Old Spaces" shows how you can make the most of your home's party potential. "Setting the Mood" reveals how to turn any table and room into a stunning party en-

vironment. "The Clever Cook" puts forth the idea that any food can become party fare—if you know how to Jazz It Up!

Each section offers easy, economical entertaining ideas that help you work with what you have. If you don't have dishes, there are suggestions for instant table settings. If you need to spark up a dull room, there are ways for putting together centerpieces from things you have around the house. Every aspect of party giving becomes a process of discovering hidden resources. You'll develop a distinct style that is really your own. And when you entertain by being yourself, there's nothing to be nervous about!

"Delight in what you have."

CHAPTER •2•

THE PARTY PLATFORM

A party is your chance to enjoy your friends and take pride in your abilities. This chapter outlines my basic party platform and offers a whole roster of techniques you can use to make your entertaining successful and fun.

I *feel* very excited to be working with you so you can become a confident host—with more style than money.

I *believe* that parties are a little bit of magic, brewed from the best ingredients: care, pleasure, and style.

I *know* that you would like to plan special get-togethers with friends. If you follow the simple guidelines in this book, you'll discover how to throw parties at which even *you* will enjoy being a guest!

Declaration of Party Principle:
STAMP OUT THE DREADS!

You know the dreads. They come up right after you hear yourself say, "I've got to have the Mosses over. I owe Sandra a dinner. It's been too long since we saw Arnold and Parker. There's no way around it. We'll have to throw a party!"

The dreads are the anxious feelings that overwhelm you when you just don't know what type of party to give or how to do it.

Why does this happen? What makes a gathering of friends and associates seem like a burden? What are you worrying about? Why do you think it is going to be so difficult?

You get into this dilemma when you don't know what you can do to make the evening a special success. You don't think you can pull off the evening the way it *should be* done. You feel as if you should have better dishes, cook fancier food, and offer more conventionally elegant surroundings.

Don't be so tough on

[5]

yourself. There are no "shoulds" when it comes to throwing a party. You and you alone are the monitor of the evening's style. Only when you take the time to recognize your own particular strengths and skills as a host can you plan a successful evening. And when you are comfortable with what you've planned, you can look forward to the evening with pleasure.

DISCOVERING YOUR NATURAL HOSTING ABILITIES

The first step to entertaining with more style than money is to become a confident, *comfortable* host. To do this, we must first understand our personal style and then find ways of extending that style when we entertain. Comfort has come to mean "to make easy," but its original meaning, "to strengthen," gives us a clue to how we can actually achieve it. We must reinforce our strengths, act out our abilities, and make life and

entertaining easy by doing what we, individually, do best.

Assess your strengths

Begin building confidence by identifying your strengths. Tune in to yourself and your environment. Recognize what you do best, what your taste is. The questionnaire in Chapter 3 will help you explore your party personality in depth and will guide you in discovering what you like best about yourself.

You'll pinpoint what you like about how you live. You'll recognize what brings you pleasure, what you find beautiful. You'll tune in to what evokes sensual sensations in you; find ways of using what you have in your house to create a strong statement of your party style.

Think about those things that are special to you. Try to identify the feelings they give you, their color and visual quality. Learn to take the colors of your favorite afghan and make them

part of the whole look of your party-ready house. Find new uses for old objects. Take an old-fashioned wash pitcher and bowl and make them the centerpiece of a Sunday brunch. Learn to make your party look an extension of what makes you feel happy, comfortable.

Develop the "as if" spirit

Extend your imagination so you see your house, its decor, even the presentation of party food "as if" they were a creative expression of your personality. Making the most of both your physical surroundings and your inner emotions is the first step to successful party giving.

Becoming a creative and imaginative host is not difficult. You don't need to be able to paint a great work of art or sculpt a marble masterpiece. Entertaining with style comes from a flexible spirit and a sensual enjoyment in the objects of everyday life. When you see a stand of tall, willowy weeds along a country road, look at them "as if" they were ensconced in a corner of your living room. When you are caught by the beauty of the sunlight on water, imagine the same sparkle created in your dining room by the play of candlelight on a glass vase. Embrace the beauty around you "as if" you could make it your own and take it home with you. You can!

BEATING THE OPPOSITION

I know that all this advice may seem impossible to accept. Throwing a party makes you nervous. You may have been entertaining for years, but you still get a headache, nervous stomach, general anxiety. You worry about the food, the mix of people, the house, your appearance. You are your own opposition when it comes to electing a comfortable entertaining attitude. The only thing to fear, really, is fear itself!

How can you beat back these fears? The "as if" spirit helps here, too.

Imagine a party "as if" you were there

- Take a couple of minutes *today* just for yourself.
- Imagine you are throwing a party.
- Set the scene very carefully.
- Create a guest list, a menu.
- Imagine yourself. What are you wearing? Make it something that is special, but comfortable. Something you can feel pretty in. Create a party that fits that mood!
- Now think of yourself "as if" you are calm, comfortable.
- Go through the process of greeting guests, introducing people.
- Notice what aspects of the party throw you— what aspects you have trouble imagining that you are doing well.
- Identify your fears. What are the worst things you think might happen? *Why do they seem so terrible?* Did dinner burn? Did you forget someone's name?
- Look for ways around these fear-provoking situations. If you are ter-

rified that dinner will burn, why are you serving something that has to be cooked at the last minute? Couldn't you cook an equally special entrée that can be served cold (and cooked a day ahead)? If you forget names, can you develop a system to get around that? Try to associate appearance or personality with names. Joanna is wearing beautiful jewelry. Jewelry = J; J = Joanna. If that doesn't work, try a clever ploy. Say, "I'll let you two take care of your own introductions. I know you'll hit it off, because you both enjoy tennis."
- Sometimes there are ways to get around a fear you cannot conquer. Since there are no rules, dinner doesn't have to be hot, attire doesn't have to be fancy, and we can find ways of taking care of party tasks that ease our anxiety.
- Continue your fantasy. Imagine talking with your guests, serving them food, saying goodbye.
- See? You got through it okay. When you ran into

a *fear*, you had the chance to find out how you could get around it. You're well on the road to gaining confidence in entertaining.

Remain Flexible!

I once gave a very fancy dinner party. All the guests were eating the first course. Downstairs, in the kitchen, the entrée was being dished up. The plates were loaded onto a dumbwaiter to be brought up to the dining room. All of a sudden there was a megaton crash! The dumbwaiter broke, plummeting the meal to the basement! I excused myself, slightly pale but well controlled. About twenty minutes later, I returned, much calmer, laughing. I'd thrown together a quick spaghetti feast to replace the lamb, and the dinner went on very successfully.

There are some disasters you can't avoid or predict. Most of the things you do worry about don't happen. If you know you can come up with a quick remedy, you won't infect your guests with your anxiety. If you stay calm and act re-sourcefully, the party will not be harmed at all. (The Off the Shelf section of "The Clever Cook" chapter will give you a whole roster of backup foods you can keep on hand to help you out in just such a "disaster.")

Use shortcuts

Throwing a party is not a solitary battle. You don't have to do everything yourself. You can rely on takeout food, help from friends. When you have a solid sense of your strengths, work to expand them. And when you iden-tify your fears, find ways around them. If cooking terrifies you, don't do it. Throw after-dinner par-ties, ask guests to bring a share of the food, or serve Italian or Chinese takeout. Enlist the help of neigh-borhood teenagers to tend bar or serve the appetizers. Get your mate to do his/her share. Have a friend co-host the party so you aren't responsible for ev-erything! Sometimes you *must* splurge and hire help—a bartender is abso-lutely necessary for large cocktail parties; a kitchen helper is useful for an elab-orate buffet or dinner. If you have no volunteers to assist you, contact a party-catering agency, a local country club, or even your favorite restaurant to provide good, professional helpers.

Don't be afraid to admit you can't do everything. The success of the party depends on the spirit you bring to it. It is more im-portant for you to be calm and confident than to cover every base yourself.

Use your emotional credit card

Whenever you are throw-ing a party, pull out your emotional credit card.

Remember a time when you were praised for some-thing you did or how you looked or acted. Build up your self-confidence by re-membering occasions that brought you a sense of pride or self-satisfaction.

I know a busy busi-nesswoman who is ter-rified of throwing parties. While we were talking one day, she suddenly under-stood that her business tal-ents were a good basis for developing entertaining skills. "You go through the same careful thought and planning for a party that I go through to get ready for a sales meeting!" That's exactly right. You can take strengths from other areas of your life and apply them to entertaining. Compliment yourself. Pat yourself on the back. Remember what you do well. Apply your natural abilities to entertaining, and you'll be amazed at the results.

Find time for yourself

Whenever you are throwing a party, plan time for yourself. There are always many things to do on the day of the party. Too often, we sacrifice ourselves for the tossed salad.

You are the most important part of your party plan. Take time to soothe your nerves, relax, and build confidence. Set aside an hour for yourself about two hours before the party is scheduled to start.

• Draw a hot tub. Pour a glass of sherry. Light a candle in the bathroom. Put on some music. And soak.

• Do deep-breathing or meditation exercises. Close your eyes. Clear your mind. Breathe deeply and slowly, exhaling evenly. Rotate your head and neck from side to side, releasing tension.

• Begin getting dressed. Put on your makeup.

• Sit quietly. Start to run through the party. Think about your guests, the topics of conversation you are interested in discussing with each one, the people whom you want to introduce to each other.

• When you are calm and feeling comfortable with yourself, it's time for the last review of the house and party layout. The salad can be tossed together at the last minute—but you should never be!

NO, NO, NO, NOAH!

We all have reasons for feeling nervous when we entertain. But in a world that seems to go two by two, the single, divorced, or widowed party-giver may feel particularly apprehensive. Whoever you are, whatever your social status, you can give good parties. It makes no difference whether you've moved to a new (and smaller) home or have only half a set of dishes or half the money you used to. The passage of time and experience will renew your entertaining confidence. That is why it is important to get your feet wet as soon as possible. To gather experience. And, with that, confidence.

I'm divorced. I really do have half my old set of china. When I was married, I entertained a lot. When I got divorced, the environment I lived in changed radically. I was afraid that people who used to come to my old house would think less of me in my smaller surroundings. Or, even worse, feel pity for me. It seems funny now, but then I wasn't sure I could make the transition from my old ways of entertaining. But my new style made the best of the new situation, and I love it!

Here are some simple guidelines that may help you begin to entertain again. They worked for me.

Don't have people over until you are calm enough to spend a whole evening without mentioning your ex! Don't pry old friends for information about your ex.

Don't put together a party made up of only old mutual friends. The situation is too loaded with memories. Invite several new people. Co-workers, members of your community group, other widow(er)s or divorced people.

Don't feel that you have to have a date. It's not necessary.

Don't ask only couples. Go for other single or unattached people. And don't worry about asking the same number of men and women.

Don't ever apologize for your "situation" or how you do things. No matter

how strong the impulse, stifle it!

Don't make the first party a big deal. Keep it simple. Start small. Late-night coffee, Sunday brunch. If you think you're going to be un-comfortable dealing with people all evening long, plan an activity. Organize a movie-going party or an outing to the beach.

And *do, do, do* ask a close friend for help. One of the mistakes newly single people make is to think of being single as being totally alone. People who are accustomed to it know that it is not an isolated state. They rely on a network of friends for support and companionship. You must learn how to extend your network, to look outside the house for personal connections.

Have a friend co-host the party, share responsibilities.

Have each guest bring a dish of food. Ask your kids for help.

Now that you are famil-iar with the basic party principle and techniques, it is time to uncover your special party personality. The questionnaire in the next chapter is designed to let you discover the type of party that you are most comfortable giving. The questionnaire sparks your imagination, makes you aware of what you think about throwing a party and how you feel about your entertaining abilities. It reveals your own per-sonal style and lets you learn to build on that. It helps you analyze your kitchen and general household setup to see what you can do within the limits of space and sup-plies. (You'll find it's a lot more than you ever guessed.) Once you get a handle on your entertain-ing inclinations, you can use that information to make an intimate dinner for two or a noisy crowd of cocktail drinkers into a smooth social occasion.

The premise of this en-tire book is that there are infinite ways to pull off a successful party. You can throw stylish, successful parties even if you are limited by space, time, or cooking abilities. Once you are aware of the kinds of parties you would like to throw, you can look through the book to uncover interesting methods of carrying out your plans—*despite* those things that you have always assumed to be limitations or liabilities. The goal is self-expression and fun!

CHAPTER •3•

DISCOVERING YOUR PARTY PERSONALITY

Your party personality is the basis of your entertaining style. It may seem to be stifled by the amount of time, money, or space you have available. It is easy to confuse the imposed inhibitions these elements create with your *actual* party-personality potential. This questionnaire seeks to help you find out exactly what your entertaining inclinations are. It reveals the circumstances that may limit your style and prepares you for exploring new ways of handling them. Then you can really let your party personality blossom!

HOW TO USE THE QUESTIONNAIRE

When answering the questions, look for your general attitudes. We are all a combination of many, often contradictory, qualities. But when you reflect on the questions, think about what you feel *most of the time*. Build your party style around personal qualities that are dominant. The goal: to recognize strengths and limitations, and to find options.

The questionnaire is divided into three sections: Assessment, Evaluation, and Conclusions.

HOW TO MAKE YOUR ASSESSMENT

- Read through the questions in the Assessment section. There is no need to write out your answers.
- Think about the issues the questions raise.
- Spend time reflecting—probe yourself, your feelings, your assumptions.
- Try to get a sense of your overall party personality.
- Examine your home's party potential.
- Identify what you en-

joy about entertaining. Look for abilities to build on.

ASSESSING YOUR COMFORT WITH GROUPS

1. Are you most at ease
   a) talking to one or two people in the course of an evening,
   b) staying home for a quiet evening,
   c) going out to a crowded bar, club, or disco, or
   d) going to a large gathering of friends?

2. How do you feel when you go to a party at someone else's house?
   a) Do you ever worry about what you'll do or say if the food isn't very good?
   b) Do you worry about getting along with new people?
   c) Do you look forward to meeting new people?
   d) Do you look forward to seeing old friends?

3. What kind of party are

you most comfortable attending?
   a) A casual party where you can sit on the floor and all the guests pitch in to help the hostess.
   b) A more structured social situation where things are more carefully planned.

ASSESSING YOUR COMFORT AS A HOST

1. When you are hosting a party, what makes you nervous?
   a) Being the center of attention.
   b) Your physical appearance.
   c) The way your house looks.
   d) The food.
   e) The possibility that your guests won't get along.

2. When you are hosting a party, what do you enjoy or feel confident about?
   a) Introducing people to each other.
   b) Your cooking.
   c) Your ability to or-

chestrate and present a party.
   d) Your conversational abilities.
   e) Your appearance.

3. When hosting a party, are you
   a) so busy making the party work that you can't join in and enjoy yourself,
   b) often caught up in long conversations,
   c) making the rounds, spending some time with each guest?

ASSESSING YOUR SENSE OF ORGANIZATION

1. How do you get organized for a party?
   a) Do you plan what you have to do each day until the party?
   b) Do you make lists: guest lists, menu and shopping lists, budgets, schedules?
   c) Do you carry around the information in your head?
   d) Do you often forget what you need to do?

2. When you plan a party, do you spend time

a) reading over cook-books,

b) jotting down menu ideas,

c) thinking about the schedule for shop-ping, cooking, cleaning?

d) Or do you leave things to the last minute?

3. Are you uncomfortable with planning and organization?

a) Does it make you more nervous?

b) Do you have some private system that you use—without being aware of it?

c) Do you spend too much time fretting over details?

d) Do you not spend enough time over them?

4. Do you plan time for yourself before a party?

a) Do you set aside time for getting dressed, relaxing, gathering your thoughts and energy?

b) Or are you rushing around, pulling your clothes on with one hand and arranging your hors d'oeuvres with the other?

ASSESSING YOUR PREVIOUS PARTY HISTORY

1. What types of parties have you given?

a) For 6 or fewer people.

b) For 6 to 12.

c) For 12 or more.

d) Buffets.

e) Cocktails.

f) Picnics.

g) Dances.

2. What was the most suc-cessful party you've given?

a) Dinner.

b) Cocktails.

c) Buffet.

d) Picnic.

e) Dance.

f) Other.

What made it so success-ful?

a) The people.

b) The food.

c) The setting.

d) Your hosting abilities.

e) All or some of these. What else?

3. What was your least suc-cessful party? Why? What went wrong?

a) Was it unsuccessful because of some un-expected disaster?

b) Was the disaster really as bad as you

felt at the time?

c) Was there a bad mix of guests?

d) Was there not enough food?

e) Was there not a com-fortable amount of space?

4. Are your guests generally

a) friends with one another,

b) the same age,

c) co-workers,

d) chosen because they have similar interests,

e) always couples,

f) always singles,

g) people who have been to your house before?

5. Do you tend to have the same people over time after time?

a) Do you ever ask peo-ple you don't know well?

b) Do you take chances mixing people of dif-ferent ages and interests?

c) Do you have friends bring a friend you don't know?

6. What is the best party you have been a guest at? Why was it special?

a) The mood.

b) The people.
c) The presentation.

ASSESSING YOUR COOKING SKILLS

1. How often do you cook dinner for yourself or your family?
a) Every day.
b) Three or more times a week.
c) Less than three times a week.
d) Hardly ever.

2. Would you consider cooking your "weekly" dishes for a party?
a) Yes.
b) If I were desperate.
c) Never.

3. Can you think of ways to "jazz up" these dishes so they'd be acceptable party fare?
a) Yes.
b) No, but I'd like to learn.
c) No, not under any circumstance.

4. How do you feel about cooking?
a) It is relaxing,
b) boring,
c) anxiety-producing.

5. Do you think you would have people over more

often if
a) you were more confident about your cooking, or
b) you didn't have to cook?

ASSESSING YOUR KITCHEN SETUP

1. Is your kitchen
a) small,
b) average, or
c) large?

2. What could you do to make it seem more versatile?
a) Increase counter space when needed.
b) Install adequate lighting on counters.
c) Get a basic supply of pots, pans, and other cooking utensils.
d) Rearrange cupboards and counters so they are uncluttered.

3. Where do you keep spices and cooking utensils?
a) Near the stove.
b) In a cupboard or drawer.
c) More than two steps from the stove.

4. Do you keep some staple and special foods on

your shelf at all times? Do you have supplies to put together a spontaneous dinner if need be?
a) Soups.
b) Canned fish and meat.
c) Canned vegetables.
d) Canned fruit and juices.
e) Pasta.

ASSESSING THE GENERAL LAYOUT OF YOUR HOUSE OR APARTMENT

1. How many rooms do you have?
a) 1
b) 2 to 4.
c) 5 or more.

2. Which of these rooms have you used for a party?
a) A 1-room studio.
b) Living room.
c) Dining room.
d) Den.
e) Bedroom.
f) Bathroom.
g) Kitchen.

3. Do you have room and facilities for a seated dinner at a table that seats
a) 2

b) 4 to 6, or
c) more than 6?

4. Have you ever created an alternative dining table
   a) using snack trays or card tables,
   b) setting dinner on a coffee table,
   c) on a picnic cloth indoors, or
   d) on the bed?

5. How many people can you accommodate on chairs or sofas?
   a) 4 or fewer.
   b) 4 to 8.
   c) 8 or more.

6. Do you have "alternate" seating available?
   a) Floor pillows.
   b) Folding chairs.
   c) Stools.

7. What is the maximum crowd you have always assumed you can accommodate for dinner?
   a) 4 or fewer.
   b) 4 to 6.
   c) More than 6.

8. For an after-dinner or cocktail party?
   a) 4 or fewer.
   b) 4 to 8.
   c) 8 or more.

9. What do you think are

the limitations of your home?
   a) Size.
   b) Lack of seating.
   c) Lack of "amenities."

10. What would you like to change or expand?
   a) The number of rooms that are "usable" for a party.
   b) The number of people you can seat for dinner.
   c) The "comfort quotient" you want for your guests.

ASSESSING YOUR PARTY HELPERS

1. Do you have willing helpers?
   a) Your roommate or lover.
   b) Your spouse.
   c) Your children.
   d) A friend.

2. Do you feel as if you should do everything yourself? Have you ever used
   a) takeout food,
   b) hired helpers, or
   c) guests to help by bringing food?

ASSESSING YOUR NATURAL STYLE

1. What decorative touches do you love in your home?
   a) Particular objects, such as a vase, afghan, or picture.
   b) The colors of your furniture or walls.
   c) The way you arrange various objects or furniture.

2. How would you characterize your home's style?
   a) Bold.
   b) Pretty.
   c) Unexpected.
   d) Countryish.
   e) Modern.
   f) Lived-in.
   g) Eclectic.

3. What kinds of additional decorative touches would you like to try?
   a) New furniture.
   b) New arrangements of old furniture.
   c) New colors.
   d) New types of accents.

4. When you imagine your dream environment, is it

a) similar to what you have, or

b) radically different?

5. What could you do—realistically—to change your environment into what you wish it were?
   a) Clear out knickknacks and clutter.
   b) Add one new, dramatic, decorative touch.
   c) Repaint or reupholster.
   d) Use space and furnishings in new ways.

HOW TO MAKE YOUR EVALUATION

Now that you have gone through the Assessment section, you should have a pretty good sense of your party personality. You have looked at your preferences for party size, your hosting abilities, your cooking skills, the party potential of your house or apartment. You have a feel for what you'd like to do as a party-giver and what restrictions or problems you face. The next step is to identify those areas that

call for new ways of doing things and to look for options and alternatives. For example:

If you have a small studio apartment, you already know that you don't have room for a traditional sit-down dinner. But you've also discovered that you like the idea of having eight friends over for a quiet evening of food and conversation. How can you combine these two seemingly disparate facts? Turn to "New Uses for Old Spaces," "Setting the Mood," and "The Clever Cook." You'll find new ways of arranging seating, using your bed and bookcase as serving tables, making good finger food for dinner, and jazzing up your apartment with inexpensive decorations.

If, on the other hand, you discover that you are terrified by the thought of having a dinner party but you really want to invite your friends over, consider the alternatives such as after-dinner gatherings, bring-your-own suppers, brunches, and pre-dinner get-togethers.

PLAN YOUR PARTY STRATEGY

The result of your reading through the Assessment section is that you are ready to make some definite decisions about the types of parties you'd like to give.

- Make specific decisions.
- Set goals.
- Choose one type of party you would like to have and schedule a date.
- List the basic needs of that party and the new ways of filling those needs. Think of new methods of serving and preparing food. Draw up potential guest lists; use your imagination to come up with clever ideas that help you accommodate guests comfortably in your home's physical layout.

Before you go on to the Conclusions, take time to identify the type of party that you are most comfortable giving. Some of us will never be at ease with a sit-down dinner. Others cannot deal with a cocktail party for sixty—no matter what our home's potential is or the degree of cooking skills we have. See if you can come up with alternatives to conventional party formats. You may, in fact, have only four dining room chairs. But is that a reason not to have ten people for dinner? No. If you want to have that many guests, you can. The only restrictions to a party's size should be your "comfort quotient." If you can cook for ten, can organize the evening easily, and would love to have that many people around for an evening, don't let the lack of chairs defeat you. The same is true if you have only a few dishes, no dining room table at all, a studio apartment, or a complete lack of cooking skills. These are not necessarily limitations. This book is chock full of easy methods for forging alternative party formats. What you must do is identify the general party format that works best for you (and in your home).

Rate Your Party Potential

1) My hosting skills are
   a) excellent.
   b) good.
   c) fair.
   d) not so hot.

2) My potential for being a good host is
   a) high.
   b) medium.
   c) shaky.

3) My home's current party potential is
   a) high.
   b) limited.
   c) seems hopeless.

4) I think I can improve my home's party potential
   a) a lot.
   b) somewhat.
   c) show me how—I haven't a clue.

5) My party cooking skills are
   a) strong.
   b) need developing.
   c) never going to exist.

6) I want to find ways to improve my party cooking skills by
   a) learning more about food and experimenting.
   b) finding out how I can "jazz up" my old standbys.
   c) learning how to use shortcuts and prepared food or takeout.
   d) finding out what kinds of parties I can throw without having to cook.

IDENTIFY YOUR STRENGTHS/ ACKNOWLEDGE YOUR LIMITATIONS

Look for ways to emphasize your abilities and to get around your limitations.

Pinpoint Your Party Personality

1) I am most comfortable throwing
   a) small parties for 6 or less.
   b) parties for about 12.
   c) big bashes where I don't have to spend much time with each guest.

2) I want to have more fun time with my friends
   a) at my house.
   b) at their house.

c) going out somewhere.

3) I imagine my party style as
   a) casual.
   b) formal.
   c) surprising.

Conclusions

Now it's time to take a stand, to commit yourself to trying out some new party formats, to making party giving a part of your life style.

I am going to give a _____ party for _____ people sometime soon.
I am going to try a new approach to preparing party food. My menu will be:

_____
_____
_____
_____
_____ .
_____
_____
_____
_____
_____
_____
_____
_____
_____
_____
_____

I am going to use the house (or apartment) in new ways.
I am going to use the living room for _____.
People will dine _____.
Seating will be set up _____.
Other rooms will be used to accommodate _____,
_____ .

CHAPTER •4•

THE PARTY WORKLIST

*A*n expansive, generous spirit *is* the most important thing to have when you entertain. Good parties are not made by the elegance of the china or the extravagance of the food. But all of us feel calmer and more confident when we know we have certain basic supplies available. If we don't have to worry about whether we have the right dishes or cooking utensils, we can spend more time finding new ways to use them.

This chapter contains a skeletal outline of the serving pieces, dishes, and kitchen utensils that make entertaining easy. The list gives you a good, foolproof basis for creating a stylish, entertaining look. I feel that a dining room is wherever you put your dinner tray—but it certainly helps if there's a dinner tray to put out!

ONE-TIME INVESTMENTS

The easiest way to set a stunning table is to begin with simple, plain white dishes. You can add to them; combine them with glass dishes or old-fashioned serving pieces. White mixes and matches with the widest variety of table decorations. White is always elegant. Food looks beautiful against white; its colors are vivid, its textures evident. There are some good-looking dishes that are dark red, blue, or black. They are dramatic. But if you put dark green vegetables and a dark brown stew on a dark blue plate, what have you got? A mystery meal!

The following list is an outline of all the different kinds of dishes that provide the basis for simple entertaining. You don't need to have each one to present a beautiful table. Pick and choose those that fit your style, needs, and budget. Look in discount stores, the five-and-ten, garage sales, and flea markets for inexpensive table settings. Keep the styles simple and versatile, and you'll put together a stun-

[21]

ning table with little cost or effort.

Table Settings

Six 12-inch-diameter white dinner plates. This oversized plate looks stunning on a table and works well as a lap plate for buffets.

Six flat salad/dessert plates, either white or glass.

Six tall, stemmed, 27-ounce oversized goblets. These work for cocktails such as Bloody Marys, all wines, fruit salad, and chocolate mousse.

Six bowls, either white or glass. These work for salad, soup, or desserts.

Six settings of flatware. Keep the pattern simple, neither ornate nor Star-Wars modern. Brightly colored handles are appealing, but limiting if they are your only set.

Six large cloth napkins, 12 inches square. Select a solid color—no prints or florals. Make them match your white dishes *or* your place mats/table-cloths.

Six place mats. Select a solid color matching the napkins. Bamboos and woven mats look smart on wood tables with peach, red, or apple-green napkins.

Six individual lap trays, to be used for buffet service or on the table. Pick a solid color in lacquer, heavy plastic, or wicker.

Three large glass platters for serving hors d'oeuvres, entrées, vegetables.

One large glass salad bowl. For use for salad course, a large salad as entrée, fruit salad, or desserts.

Six white cups and saucers. They all do not have to be the same size and shape. Even six different patterns on white provide an attractive, eclectic look.

Six white votive candles and glass holders.

Six small glass bud vases.

Extra touches for the table

Although not strictly nec-essary, the following list of items for the table helps set a festive tone and gives you additional flexibility in creating a wide variety of party looks.

Six individual glass salt and pepper cellars.

Six individual, round, mousse-style rame-kins. These small, straight-sided dishes are good for butter, any condiment, des-sert puddings, and in-dividual sauce containers.

Six small hors d'oeuvres trays—4 by 6 inches—large enough to hold finger food and rest glass on when guests are standing. Solid color or glass or lucite.

Six sets of chopsticks.

Six napkin rings.

Six 2-inch-diameter clay pots and saucers.

One wicker bread basket.

Six shallow, flat wicker baskets, 6 inches in diameter, for serving crackers, dips, hors d'oeuvres, nuts.

One wicker wine bottle holder.

Six small glass dip bowls.

Kitchen Supplies for Food Preparation

Three knives of various sizes.
One cutting board.
Three mixing bowls—nested—white or light ceramic so they can be used on the table, too.
One grater.
One garlic press.
Four wooden spoons.
One spatula.
One can opener.
One long fork.
Strainer.
Measuring cups and spoons.
Pot holders.
Dish towels.

Extra touches

Blender—an essential tool for the shortcut gourmet and the non-cook alike.
Electric mixer—for desserts, whipped cream, and egg whites. It is much easier than elbow grease.
Food processor. There are those who swear by it, but just remember, the great chefs of France did pretty well without it!
Wire whisk.

Timer.
Salad spinner.

Supplies for Cooking and Serving Food

One large lasagna-style pan, 9 by 13 inches.
Two large casseroles with lids. For use from oven to table.
Three trivets/hot pads of wood or glass or tile—plain, no pattern.
One meat loaf pan for small casseroles and other uses.
One large soup/spaghetti pot with lid.
One roasting pan with rack.
Two frying pans—9 inches and 12 inches in diameter—of cast iron or other heavy metal.
Two saucepans, one smaller than the other so they can be used as a double boiler.
Glass pie plate.

Extra touches

Six "boat-shaped" ramekins for cooking and serving individual portions as entrée or first course.
Six large scallop shells

for hot or cold first courses.
Fondue pot or chafing dish for cooking at the table.
Wok.
Fish poacher.
Skewers for shish kebabs as hors d'oeuvres or entrées.

"There's no holding you back now."

CHAPTER •5•

THE PARTY INDEX

So you want to throw a party. Where do you start? There are so many different kinds of get-togethers that you could arrange. How can you decide what's best for you?

Perhaps you are nervous about entertaining. Or your options may be limited by time, money, or space. Whatever your situation is, you should plan a party that fits your abilities and works with (not against) the obstacles you have.

Look for a new kind of party experience. Think beyond the standard dinner party. Try to make your mark as an original hostess. Come up with an entertainment that is distinctive.

Whatever your circumstance, you're in luck. This chapter explores many different types of parties. We'll look at dinner and cocktail parties in a new light.

Read through the suggestions. See what may work for you. The Party Questionnaire should have helped you realize your party style and potential. Now you can focus on specific party formats. Each category is referenced to the appropriate sections in the book which provide tips on cooking, decorating, and using your home in innovative ways.

CHOOSING A PARTY FORMAT

When you begin to plan a party, ask yourself the following questions:

- Do I want to provide a complete meal? Do I want to cook it? Do I want to provide takeout food? Have guests contribute to the meal?
- Do I want to have people over in the evening? On the weekend, when I have time during the day to prepare? During the week, when I have very little time to get ready?
- If I have people over during the week, what

can I do to make sure that I have enough time to prepare for the party and relax, too? Should I have people over for cocktails and hors d'oeuvres? For after-dinner drinks? For dessert?

• If I want to give a large party, what format is best? How much room do I have? Can I give an afternoon open house? A late-morning brunch? An evening cocktail party? Should I stagger the hours?

• If I don't have much furniture, how can I feed people comfortably? Can I give a picnic—indoors or out?

• How can I master entertaining skills? By starting small? Do I go for a quiet supper for two, a small group of six for after-dinner cheer? Or do I want to jump in with both feet and ask a big crowd? Do I work best in a sink-or-swim situation?

As you can see, there are a lot of options. Let's take a brief look at each. See what sounds best for you.

GENERAL OR-GANIZATIONAL GUIDELINES

The work, spirit, and execution of all kinds of party plans rely on the same basic techniques. Whatever you're planning, you need to get acquainted with the guidelines listed below.

PARTICULAR PARTIES

Dinner Parties

A dinner party is a gathering of people to share a meal. That is the only generalization you can make about it. It may be seated or buffet, a banquet or a picnic, elegant or casual, gourmet or country fare, intimate or bustling. The choice is yours. You must decide on the most suitable format for your environment and the right style for your party personality. Following is a list of the various places in the book where these alternatives are explored.

Menu

Cocktail Parties

There are afternoon cock-
tail parties, early-evening
or late-night versions, too.
They can be festive one-
drink occasions. You may
want to provide a whole
meal or just an array of
tasty munchables. Select
whatever format works
with your budget and
style.

The Party Index

The information that is listed above for dinner and cocktail parties can be applied to any entertaining situation. For brunch, lunch, a picnic, or tea, the special looks and styles are all useful. Below is a list of several other types of parties, with references to illustrations and text, that may spark your imagination.

"Adopt an expansive spirit."

CHAPTER •6•

NEW USES FOR OLD SPACES

We all have complaints about the plaints about the size and setup of our house or apartment. We could give gracious parties *if* . . . if we had a larger living room, a bigger dining table, a more workable kitchen, more dishes, more chairs, more glasses . . . The list of reasonable complaints goes on and on! Believe me, I know.

I don't have a dining room at all. My kitchen is better suited to boiling water than baking cakes.

But I refuse to let matters of "geography" hamper my party spirit!

To overcome the seeming limitations of my apartment, I have applied equal parts of enthusiasm, imagination, and personal taste. I let my spirits soar within the confines of my home's inherent nature.

This is what I want to help you do, too. I want you to get excited about putting your imagination into high gear.

You can develop new ways of entertaining in your home.

You can make the most of your party potential.

You can beat back the physical and spiritual boundaries that keep you from making the most of your cramped situation!

This chapter contains suggestions for converting all the rooms in your home into party-ready environments. Designed to spark your imagination, they should help you uncover new ways of entertaining that fit your personality *and* your home.

There are no ironclad "do's" or "don't's." I have evolved certain techniques through trial and error. They work for me. I offer them to you to accept or not. But I do urge you to embrace the spirit of these techniques—to begin to understand that there are no limits to your entertaining abilities except those that are self-imposed.

CREATING ILLUSIONS OF SPACE

There are a few basic techniques that can make any room seem more spacious. Read over the list below. Then think about how your living room, dining area, bedroom, kitchen, and bath are set up when you give a party. Ask yourself: "What could I do to change the feeling of space in these rooms? How could I make them more comfortable? Which of these suggestions are useful to me?"

• Before a party, remove all knickknacks, magazines, small objects from tables, dresser tops, shelves. Clear surfaces so guests have room for ashtrays, glasses, and plates. If you want to keep certain objects out, let them make a strong visual statement of the party decor and mood.

• Keep the corners of the rooms clear. Put away small objects that you've stored or stashed under tables. Keep sight lines as uncluttered as possible.

• Arrange seating so that it is against the walls or in definite L or U shapes. Whenever possible, create at least two distinct seating areas (in one room or in different rooms) so guests have room to move around from group to group.

• Use mirrors along walls in narrow rooms to create reflected space.

• Highlight one object in each room—a pretty, architectural feature, a painting, a plant, a centerpiece, a piece of furniture, or even a colorful afghan. Have it be a big, bold statement.

• Don't fight a room. It has its own "feel." Don't try to mask an "ugly" feature temporarily. If there are exposed pipes, keep them in the shadows—don't paint them red! If a wall is peeling, keep it darkened—don't tack a piece of cloth over it. When decorating, don't try to make a small, low-ceilinged room more glamorous by stuffing it full of busy, fancy furniture. Heavy objects will only make the room seem smaller, less satisfactory.

• When giving a large party in a small area, move furniture to provide maximum floor space (or remove it). When giving a small party, group furniture into cozy, intimate arrangements, making the togetherness seem intentional, not inevitable.

• Whatever you do, in any room, make it seem purposeful, well thought out. If you appear in control of the space, the result will be a bold statement that puts guests at ease.

How to Create Illusions of Space with Lights

• Keep lighting around edges of rooms. Light plants from below. Light baseboards with incandescent tube lights for a floating-in-space illusion. Place spots behind sofas and chairs for a diffused glow. Keep center of room dim or candlelit.

• Highlight glass étagères, shelves, with spots from above. Use the sparkle and airiness of glass—whether from a table, shelf, or large bowl—to provide a see-through illusion.

• Divide space with light. If sitting, talking, and then dining all in one room, create the feeling of two rooms by lighting only one area at a time. Have cocktails and hors d'oeuvres while in "living" area. Light candles, point indirect spots toward area. Cast shadow on "dining" area. When ready to eat, light candles in dining space, turn spots to backlight area, blow out candles in "living" area, and plunge it into darkness.

• When using "alternative spaces" for entertaining, such as the kitchen or bath, never use fluorescent or overhead fixtures. They are too connotative of the room's usual function. Instead, bring in candles. In short, light these rooms as you would a conventional party room. That way, you create a more convincing and natural party space.

OLD SPACES ... NEW USES

So you're giving a party. How will you ever fit everyone into the living room? There are not enough chairs, too little floor space.

Well, you'll just have to eliminate some guests, scale down. You can't have those new neighbors over this time ... again. Right? Wrong!

You have a whole houseful of untapped space. The bedroom, the kitchen, the living room, even the second bathroom can be turned into a usable entertaining area. Somewhere along the line, the idea got planted in our brains that guests should not enter the "private" areas of the home. Yet those "other" rooms are gold mines of entertaining space. And they are not places of last resort—or part of an unhappy compromise. They are full-fledged, party-ready, elegant, efficient entertaining areas. They're just waiting for someone to use them.

Basic Principles of Converting Old Spaces

• Remove all items from a room or area that are connotative of its usual function. For example, all cosmetics, clothes, and dressing-table supplies should be taken out of the bedroom. Clear off dresser tops, alarm clock, slippers, etc. Keep kitchen counters and surfaces clear, clean, and free of bulky appliances.

• Don't hesitate to rearrange the furniture. Plan each room as if it were a "living" room. Think of the flow of traffic and seating.

• Make all themes, lighting, decor, centerpieces, visual touches, and music unified from room to room. Create a feeling of whole-house unity.

• And last ... never, never apologize or make excuses to your guests about your unusual use of space. You can make it work for everyone if you feel comfortable and confident that it works for you.

ing food is to set it up for buffet service. This is convenient when there is no separate dining area and

the living room is too small to accommodate both the buffet and the eating guests.

CONVERTING THE BEDROOM

The bedroom has all kinds of alternative possibilities. The dresser tops make suitable buffets or bars; the bed itself can be used for dining or sitting; chairs can be brought in to make cozy seating arrangements; and the floor space can accommodate a small crowd for cocktails. To make it work, just follow these simple steps:

Movable Feasts

Bedroom dining is not a scheme for sensual suppers, although it is certainly a good idea. For seated dinners or buffet spreads, the bedroom makes a party room.

Boudoir buffet

The second way you can use your bedroom for serv-

To convert your bed into a dining table:
- *Cover mattress with solid-colored, smooth, fitted bedcover.*
- *Set mattress with wicker trays with raised sides. Have place settings for each guest contained on trays. This includes one large plate, a 27-ounce goblet, flatware, napkins or checkered dish towel, salt and pepper plus one small bud vase with a flower.*
- *Surround the mattress with oodles of comfy floor pillows. If you are so inclined, you can purchase folding floor chairs with backs—but no legs. They are available at a variety of wicker shops, home furnishings stores, or garden shops.*
- *Prepare food that is easily eaten with the fingers—artichokes; cheeses and fruit; chicken; assembly-line, make-your-own sandwiches; soups in mugs. Stay away from food that requires cutting with a sharp knife or that is drippy or heavily sauced.*
- *Keep the wine cooling in a tin bucket on the floor. Place it in a wicker basket, tie a bright red ribbon around it, or spray-paint it to make it more festive.*
- *Put a centerpiece on the "fourth" side of the mattress. Use a large vase or wicker basket. Fill it with greenery, branches, bark, or autumn leaves. Use anything that doesn't need water!*

Variation:

• *If you have a bed board or any firm surface to place over mattress, remove bedspread, put down board, cover with pad and then a beautiful tablecloth. Set places as you would on any tablecloth.*

• *For a relaxing or intimate dinner for two, you can dine in bed.*

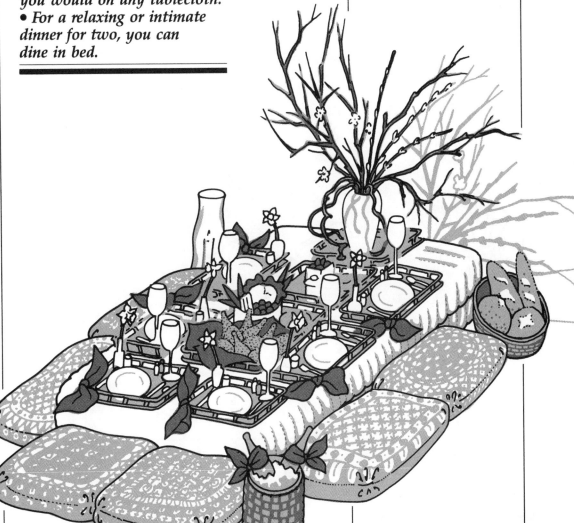

To convert your dresser into a buffet:

- *Clear off all dresser tops and small bedroom tables.*
- *Protect wood surfaces with a waterproof sheet of plastic.*
- *Cover surfaces with long runners, tablecloths, or place mats. Coordinate coverings so that dresser tops and tables look unified. Beware of draping long tablecloths ... you want to cover the entire dresser, but don't let cloth drag on floor. One wrong step, and dinner will be pulled underfoot.*
- *You may use the mattress surface for an additional serving area if dresser and table tops are not big enough. Place all food in flat trays or on board covered with decorative fabric.*
- *Plan routing carefully. Walk through setup, making sure there is room to get in and out easily and that the buffet is arranged logically.*
- *Do not serve any drinks in buffet area.*

General Guidelines

- Have a set of party bedcovers. Get tailored, tight-fitting mattress and box spring coverings with matching square pillows. Eliminate anything that looks too frilly or bedroomy. Make bed enticing for lounging. Consider covering bed with fabric that matches walls so it blends into room and does not stand out.
- Remove footboard (or entire frame) or put mattress and box spring on floor.
- Put food or drink in room, even if not strictly necessary. It will pull people into the area and spread out the crowd.
- Set up seating in room. Have big bolsters on bed for sitting. Bring in chairs and small table to create a seating alcove if room allows.
- Put pillows on the floor.

Bedroom Bar

One of the surest ways to get your guests to spread the party out into the bedroom is to put the bar in there! When you are having a large group of guests over for cocktails or late-night revelry, you can make this conversion very easily. If you have a second bathroom off the bedroom, consider using it as part of the bar setup, too. See page 39 for details. For information on how to set up a bar and ideas for alternative drinks, see "Liquid Assets," page 149.

To convert your dresser into a bar:

- *Set all bottles, glasses, and condiments on trays to protect dresser top.*
- *Decant liquor. Keep service simple.*
- *Put backup supplies of soda, ice, wine, etc., into ice-filled, galvanized tin in corner of room.*
- *Offer one type of glass for all beverages. The 27-ounce goblet is elegant and versatile.*

CONVERTING THE BATHROOM

If you are lucky enough to have a second bathroom, you have the setting for an instant bar. All you need is a tub, a candle, and a fifth of cleverness. Let's see how they can be put together. Here's "before" and "after."

To convert your bathroom into a bar:

* *Remove all toilet articles from sight—soap, washcloths, shampoo, shavers, cosmetics, Q-Tips—everything!*
* *Remove area rugs.*
* *Scrub the room to high-gloss perfection.*
* *Remove shower curtain or tie it back with ribbons. Cover chrome shower-curtain rod*

[39]

with ribbon, crêpe paper, or plastic rod cover in a color that matches bathroom walls.
- *Use low wattage pink lights overhead, and oodles of candles.*
- *Line the bottom of the tub with plastic trash bags. Fill to top with ice cubes.*
- *Insert wine, soda, beer in ice. Tie festive ribbons on neck of wine bottles. Open wine, reinsert cork. Have beer in screw-off tops.*
- *Decorate the ice in the tub with gold glitter. Plant votive candles around the rim of the tub, in the ice, or put some greenery or fresh flowers around the bottles, or add color with red berries, confetti, streamers, shells, grapes, or a massive folding fan along the back wall of the tub. Bring in palms.*
- *Line sink basin with plastic. Fill with ice for drinks. Put sign on faucets: "Don't turn me on!" If sink is too small, or if you need to use it for counter space, put ice buckets on the ice in tub.*
- *Arrange general bar supplies—lemons, limes, openers, corkscrews, napkins, and stacks of glasses—on counter and shelves around ice-filled sink; OR cover sink with a flat board, drape with a shimmery white cloth, and use as table space for bar supplies. Ice buckets can rest on ice in tub; OR bring in snack table and set up next to sink.*
- *Keep toilet seat permanently closed. Place heavy basket filled with greens, flowering twigs and branches, cut flowers, or a pot of tulips or daffodils.*
- *Place candles around bar supplies, on back of toilet, on shelves.*

CONVERTING THE LIVING ROOM

If you have a small living room and want to make it work for greeting, seating, or feeding guests, there are a few simple techniques you can use that will create a completely fresh look. Just remember to keep a grand, expansive feeling about your conversions of old spaces to new uses, and you will be able to pull off anything!

Greeting Guests

The crunch at the front door when guests first arrive can ruin the mood of a party. You feel frazzled and out of control, and your guests think they're entering chaos. But what can you do if you don't have a foyer, or the living room furniture crowds the front door?

- *For instant closet space, invest in a collapsible coat rack.*
- *Provide a square of black shag carpet for boots and a clay pot or tube for umbrellas if the weather is bad.*
- *After guests arrive, cover up area with a folding screen. Note: Screens can easily be made by stapling cotton fabric or sheets to panels formed from canvas stretchers. Hinge panels together and you've got a handsome, sturdy screen.*

Feeding Guests

If you don't have a dining table, are not inclined to dine in the bedroom, or are already using it for a bar, there are a lot of ways to feed a hungry crew in the living room. To create instant dining facilities, consider:

2. Increasing size of tables by laying larger board over table, covering with cloth.

1. Sawhorses with folding table tops.

3. Snack trays and cafe trays that hold two place settings.

[42]

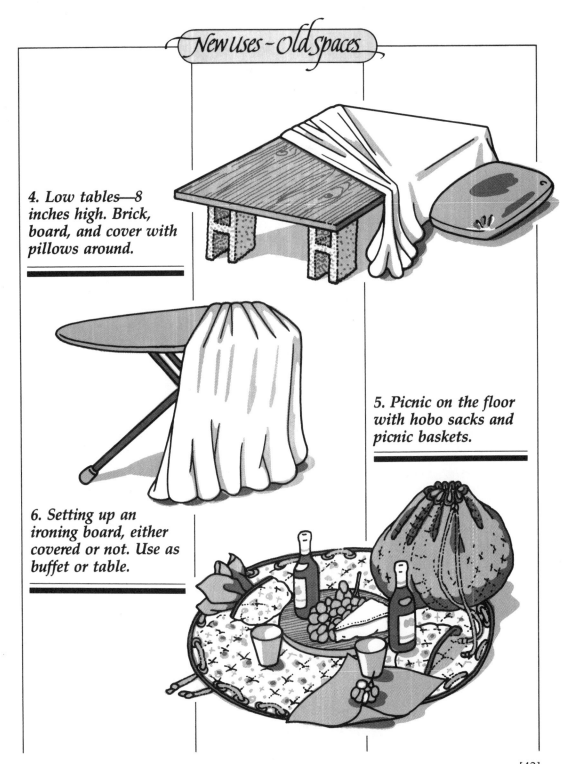

4. Low tables—8 inches high. Brick, board, and cover with pillows around.

5. Picnic on the floor with hobo sacks and picnic baskets.

6. Setting up an ironing board, either covered or not. Use as buffet or table.

7. Lap trays and buffet on desk, bookshelf, and mantel.

Seating Guests

To provide more room for seating guests, you have to rearrange furniture, create some "instant chairs," and find new ways of placing guests into comfortable, functional groupings.

• *Create two seating areas. This lets guests change conversations easily and gives a feeling of space and mobility to any party.*
• *Depend on small, stackable bamboo tables, floor pillows, and folding chairs. Pillows can be stacked and stored easily when not in use. They are comfortable, and you can even make them from fiberfill and two king-size pillow cases. Folding chairs are often unattractive, but those of natural wood, bright-colored metal, or lucite look good and are easy to store. If you think your guests will be uncomfortable on the floor, use folding chairs, stools, or director's chairs.*
• *If you are really short of furniture, create benches for sitting. Place them in a corner or against a wall so guests can lean back. Instant benches can be made from two wire "milk bottle holders," sprayed black, and a*

plank of 12-inch-wide pine board, sprayed black. Top with pillows. Easy to store when not in use. If you prefer, use redwood picnic table benches. Scrub clean. Top with pillows.
• *Clear off bookcase shelves and use for serving coffee, dessert, or appetizers.*
• *Soften lighting. Drape table lamps with sheer China silk remnants. Use candles.*
• *Create arrangements on top shelf of bookcase and coffee table. Set up a collection of bud vases on a tray. Use greenery and one or two flowers to create drama— economically.*
• *Set up bar on tea tray. Have extra wine or liquor on floor in cooler.*

CONVERTING YOUR KITCHEN

The kitchen? Ugh! That land of dirty dishes? The last bastion of chaos before a party! How could you ever use that den of spilled spices and chopped parsley as an active party room?

Very nicely. For a serve-yourself buffet of hors d'oeuvres, soup, salad, or entrée. A kitchen buffet can be both visually pleasing and practical.

General Guidelines

• *Clear off all counters. Put away large appliances, mops, kitchen cleaners, liquid soap, cleanser.*
• *Make lighting soft—place candles and plants on counter, not overhead.*
• *If there is a double sink, put dirty dishes in one side and then cover with cutting board*

that rests securely over sink; or throw a pretty, oversized napkin or dish towel over them.
• Set out dishes, and flatware standing in ceramic vases, on counters, or individual lap trays, already set.
• Do not serve any drinks in the kitchen when using it for a buffet.
• The key to serving from the kitchen is to choose the right menu and set the food out in the most attractive way.

Hors d'oeuvres

Hot, but not in the oven—cheese, spreads, rarebit dip on stove, soup served in mugs, spareribs or curried shrimp arranged in skillet with toothpicks.

Salad

An assembly-line salad works well. Fill sink with ice. Place glass salad bowl into ice. Fill with greens, garnish with tomatoes and shredded carrots for color. Place add-a-flavor ingredients on counter: chopped avocados, scallions, cheese, mushrooms, anchovies, nuts, mandarin oranges, ham, turkey; even fish, chicken, or cold duck for entrée salads. Have dressings in pitchers for easy pouring. Serve oil and vinegar, creamy herb, sesame, lemon dressings.

Entrées

For a complete kitchen buffet, including a main course, choose dishes that are cooked and served in individual portions: chicken curries, gumbos, stews, casseroles, rice dishes, vegetables kept warm in steamers over simmering water.

CONVERTING YOUR STUDIO APARTMENT INTO A BACK LOT

All the problems and pressures of entertaining in a cramped space are multiplied tenfold in studio apartments. Nonetheless, more and more of us find studios to be the easiest and most affordable style of living. But we don't want living in a small space to make our social life small, too!

General Guidelines

• *When setting up a studio apartment, keep entertaining needs in mind. Have bed well tailored with throw pillows to look like a sofa. Use as many built-ins/hidden storage areas as possible. Use space under bed, sofa, and counters for storage. Keep colors subdued. Use bright colors for accents; on walls and furniture, they close in space. Go for one big arrangement or decorating touch. This makes space seem more important. Stay away from little accessories that clutter your limited space. Choose furniture with multiple uses—desk/tables, benches that work for seating or coffee tables. Use screens to demark areas within room. Apply lighting guidelines from page 32 in this chapter.*

• *Whenever possible, create a sharp distinction between the living, sleeping, and kitchen areas of the studio. While all areas should be comfortable for guests, the feeling of distinct areas increases an illusion of space.*

• *Rely on folding furniture that can be brought out when needed and stored easily: folding chairs, table tops, metal sawhorses, screens, snack trays.*

• *Make bed trim and upholstered. Provide bolster pillows. Use for seating.*

• *Screen off kitchen.*

• *Use desk and dresser for buffet service.*

• *Set up bar on tea cart.*

• *Use small stools and tables for additional seating and eating space.*

• *Place some furniture on a diagonal. This provides texture and creates an illusion of space.*

• *Eliminate small plants and arrangements.*
Go for one dramatic plant. Soften with
flowers around soil. Create upward light
with candles.

To Accommodate a Large Gathering

• *Arrange a party with staggered hours. Issue the first fifteen invitations for five to seven p.m., the next ten for six-thirty to eight, the last fifteen for seven-thirty to nine-thirty. Do it by alphabetical order of names.*

• *If serving food, rely on takeout, deli, and other prepared items. You have enough to juggle without trying to get food ready!*

• *Use the studio for a gathering of twenty-five people. Serve everyone drinks, easily munchable hors d'oeuvres. Then move the second phase of the party to an outside location—a movie, the park, a tailgate picnic, a disco or restaurant. You can make it your treat, or indicate on the invitations that it's a Dutch-treat situation. Your gift is the cocktail hour and the time and organization necessary to put it all together.*

THE EFFICIENT KITCHEN

Has there ever been a kitchen that was truly large enough? Except for those tantalizing pictures in glossy magazines, we rarely get to see such a splendid sight. However, there is a lot we can do to make our kitchens ample enough for preparing grand party feasts.

Basically, it takes organization and the time to sort through crowded cupboards and cluttered counters. An efficient kitchen is one that works with us, not against us. Now, this may seem elementary, but how many of us have to move the rarely used roasting pan out from in front of the six extra mixing bowls we got last Christmas to get to the blender base that has somehow lodged itself at the very back of the top cupboard shelf?

We don't need this kind of hassle—or the problem of stuffing everything back into the cupboard after we are done—when we are getting our party food ready.

Likewise, how many

times have you had to abandon your delicately simmering sauce to sort through your spices until you found what you needed for that last-minute flavoring touch? These hassles make us believe we can't entertain or cook as easily as we'd like to.

Preparing party food can be the most stressful part of entertaining. We should do everything we can to make the most of our kitchen facilities.

Get the kitchen ready for cooking your party menu:

Organizing Stove Area

• Have spices within handy reach, but not too close—heat can sap their flavor.
• Have a drawer or handy container near the stove with all wooden spoons, spatulas, and sharp knives.
• Have hot pads and trivets within arm's length.
• If a cupboard is above the stove, store pots and pans there, *not* food.
• If you have space on the stove's surface, place

heat-resistant ceramic or wooden cutting board there for convenient cutting and dicing.

Organizing the Counter Area

• If counter space is at a premium, put away cookbooks and appliances until you need them. Keep large-sized paper towel roll nearby.
• Have a lucite cookbook stand available so you can follow your recipes easily—without holding open the book with one hand and sifting the flour with the other.
• Whenever possible, store utensils and pans used to prepare food—such as sifters, measuring cups, mixing bowls —in the cupboard directly above the counter you work on.
• Increase counter area by installing fold-down counter top or bringing in counter-high tables to help you while you're preparing food. Set up your ironing board (covered) for more counter space!

Arranging the Refrigerator

To get your party food out efficiently and easily, you have to be able to use your refrigerator to maximum capacity.

• Before you begin preparing your party food, defrost the freezer. This will give you more freezer storage space, more efficient cooling throughout, and will freshen the air in the fridge itself.
• Remove all food from the refrigerator that does not absolutely have to be kept cold. Many of us store bread, cereals, catsup, mustard, etc. Clear these items out.
• Adjust inner shelves so that you have enough height to accommodate the large cooking and serving pieces you may be storing.
• Try arranging all foods needed for each party dish on one shelf. Far too often we forget a garnish or a special addition because we simply didn't see it when we went to take out the ingredients.
• Wash and cut up all

[51]

vegetables and salad supplies ahead of time. Keep them fresh in plastic bags. Place paper towels in bags with leaves of lettuce to absorb excess moisture.

• Store mushrooms, green peppers, and potatoes in paper bags, not in plastic. Paper lets the food breathe and prevents it from becoming soggy.

Getting Ice Ready to Go

If you have an ice maker, or make your own in trays, prepare ice by putting it in large plastic bags. The bags will be easy to use for filling up small ice buckets or large tubs. Ice doesn't get frosty, and you don't have to struggle with ice trays while the party's going on. If you need the freezer to store dessert, keep ice cool in a portable styrofoam chest.

TRICKS FOR PREPARING A LOT OF FOOD IN A SMALL AREA

• One key to preparing a lot of party food in a small kitchen is the selection of the right kind of menu.

—Never cook anything that requires last-minute preparation.

—Plan on serving at least two cold dishes. For example, cold hors d'oeuvres and a salad, or a cold entrée and a cold dessert. These dishes don't take up precious oven or stove-top space and can often be prepared well ahead of time.

—Depend on some prepared or canned foods so that you don't have to cut, wash, or cook everything that is served. Canned antipasto ingredients, garnishes for salads— such as olives, anchovies, or chick peas—frozen cheese soufflés, or canned tomato sauces are examples of the kind of quality food that you can make from supplies right off the shelf. (For more details, see page 135 for a whole roster of Off the Shelf recipes.)

• Once you have set your menu, there is still the problem of getting everything ready to be cooked. Prepare each ingredient ahead of time. If you know that the beef stew requires chopped onions, carrots, and potatoes, that the salad greens must be washed, crisped, and torn into bite-size pieces, and that the chocolate needs to be grated for a dessert topping, do all these prep jobs at once. Store each recipe's ingredients in an airtight container in the fridge. They are ready to use when needed. You won't have to juggle counter space while you're trying to keep your eye on the browning stew meat.

• Assembling cooked dishes for the table is also difficult when there isn't much counter space.

—Try to cook dishes that can be taken directly from the stove to the table. Make it a point to have several casseroles, big and small, rustic and fancy, to help carry this plan out.

• Never begin a party with dirty dishes in the

sink. You'll regret it later!

• For seated dinners, have the first course on the table when guests are seated.

• Consider serving the main course yourself. Stack plates in front of you — Thanksgiving style! It is very difficult to bring plates already prepared from the kitchen if there's limited counter space. You can, of course, have food passed around the table from guest to guest, but some dishes are better suited to this than others. Never do this with anything that must be sliced or cut.

• Use a rolling tea cart to hold salad bowls, the cheese and fruit course, or dessert plates and coffee cups. There's nothing as convenient as a mobile counter!

• Once the meal's been eaten and it's time to return all the dishes to the kitchen, you can run into serious trouble with teetering stacks of plates, piles of half-empty serving dishes. It looks terrible. Makes serving dessert difficult.

And can cause a dangerous avalanche.

—If you don't have a dishwasher, fill large pot with hot, soapy water. Drop all flatware inside to soak. Stack rinsed plates in sink filled with water. Set glasses on edge of stove or on large tray. Fill cooking pots and casserole with water and stack them in oven. Out of sight if not out of mind.

—Don't take time to wash the dishes. You should not be away from your guests for that length of time. And you should be having fun yourself!

CHAPTER •7•

SETTING THE MOOD

You can orchestrate the mood of a party by creating breathtaking table settings and centerpieces. Bold, inventive setups tell your guests the spirit and style you have planned for the evening (or morning or afternoon).

When you throw a party, feed your eyes first! Let your fantasies become real. Experience the joy of translating the special qualities you want your party to have into a real-life statement. There are boundless resources in your home and in nature that you can use to make any table setting, centerpiece, or arrangement a powerful expression of your party personality.

A table is not just a groaning board! It is a canvas. The linens, dishes, serving pieces that you use can affect the food you serve, making it look exotic, rustic, elegant. Even making it taste better!

A centerpiece or arrangement is not just a vase of expensive flowers.

It can capture the grandest, boldest, and most beautiful qualities you want to bring to your party. You are surrounded by objects that can be used. The beauty of sand or stone, of rusty autumn leaves, of one perfect anemone, of terra-cotta pots, of glass or flame or wild flowers, can bring surprise and impact to a table.

To learn how to set your own mood, you must tune in to the things around you that intrigue you, provoke your senses, please your eye. Find the elements in nature, in art, in your home, that are useful components of table settings and centerpieces. Recall memories of sensual environments. Remember the last time you walked on a beach or through the countryside. Identify the things about those environments that seemed beautiful to you. Look everywhere for inspiration.

• Examine room settings in magazines, movies, TV shows, or department stores. Learn to be critical of them. Look for what pleases you. Identify what you do *not* like. Learn to discriminate.

• Think of table settings and arrangements as combinations of colors, textures, and shapes. If you love certain colors, find foods, table settings, and objects for an arrangement that uses those colors.

• Look through your house. Find those items that you love. Dig them out of closets and corners. Think of them as part of a table setup. Think of what other objects, plants, flowers, and candles you could use with them. You may be inspired by your grandmother's Victorian china cup, a vase, an old carved box with a lid, a collection of seashells, even an old china doll. There are no NOs. Only endless possibilities!

Getting in the Mood

• Develop a visual sense of rhythm. When you set a table and create a centerpiece, you want to evoke a sense of movement. You don't want a static, stiff look any more than you want a static, stiff party.

On a table, rhythm comes from a pattern formed by the long line of a goblet stem, the round arc of a salad plate, the complementary curve of a dinner plate, broken up by the arresting fold of a napkin, all held together by the place mat or tablecloth beneath.

In a centerpiece, rhythm comes from the tension between the arrangement and its container, the shapes of the objects, their height, spread, color.

• Go for simplicity. Let the centerpiece be the star of the table. Make the table setting complement it, not fight it.

But don't think small. Tiny dabs of halfhearted decorations are useless; they have no impact, lack the element of boldness that seizes the attention and sets a tone. Don't spread out your arrangements hoping to make them look like more. That only has the opposite effect.

When creating a unique table setting, follow through. If you use rustic place mats with an old-fashioned print, keep the theme going by using wood or crockery condiment and serving dishes, a centerpiece of country grasses. Don't make a timid statement.

• Make the food you serve fit the table setting you create. The entire evening should be presented as a unified image. Country dishes call for country food—it can be Southern or French, depending on your inclination, but make it appropriate.

LIGHTING THE WAY

No single item can change the appearance of a room, its feeling of beauty, drama, or space, more than lighting. A party can be destroyed or created by the lighting that is used.

General Principles of Party Lighting

• Begin a party with the lights up. Lights should be fairly bright when you are greeting guests, making introductions. People like to be seen when they enter a party room. They have made an effort with their appearance and want a chance to show it off.
• Make sure all stairs, driveways, lawn areas are well lit all the time.
• Once conversation has blossomed and the first drinks have been served, dim the lights slightly. People are a lot like plants. They respond to light, change their appearance in direct reaction to it. However, except for glorious, golden sunlight, people look best in subtle, indirect light. They feel less exposed, more intimate and warm.
• Don't light candles during daylight. But always have a bountiful supply for the whole evening.
• Keep the dining areas softly lit, but not dark.

Your guests will want to know what they're eating, and you want them to appreciate the appearance of the food.
• Use lighting (spots or candles) to draw attention to centerpieces, plants, or flowers in every room.

How to Prepare Party Lighting

• Install three-way bulbs wherever possible. This gives you maximum flexibility.
• Install dimmer switches on overhead lights. Dimmers may be installed on table lamps, too. Gradually lower lights over the course of the evening.
• Use amber or pink bulbs in all fixtures to cast a cozy, soft glow.
• Keep all bulbs dust-free.
• Put a dot of perfume on bathroom bulb—its warmth will infuse the room with a sweet smell.
• For extra drama, line lampshades with pink gel, or drape pastel China silk scarves over shades.

• To disguise ugly overhead fixtures, cover with inexpensive paper Chinese lanterns, or drape two "runners" at right angles over light.

Candles

Candles are the easiest, most visually pleasing lighting trick you can use to set a party mood. They are fast, inexpensive ways of highlighting special features in any room. They can focus attention or create a feeling of mystery. Any space becomes more magical. Small areas seem to have a gentle quality. The sharp boundaries of a space are softened or obscured. It's hard to believe that there was a time when candles were the only light available. But now they are a romantic, elegant alternative.

I am candle-crazy. I don't think you can have too many. That's why I cluster them around centerpieces, on the mantel, on individual serving trays, by bed and bath! As with all "arrangements," there are some common-sense guidelines to remember.

• *Avoid sticking two long tapers into tall silver candlesticks and placing one at each end of a mantel or on either side of a centerpiece. How dull!*

• *Combine groups of four to six candles. I like to use candles that are the same color. They can be different shapes and sizes. If they are not, I place them on different levels. Raise one up a little on a lacquered box, another on a small black tray. Let the eye move from one to the other, up and down, sensing the texture of the arrangement. (Remember, get dripless candles!)*

• *Make candle holders from found objects. Use seashells of various sizes, ceramic or glass condiment bowls, mini liqueur bottles from the airlines, or vases.*

Carve out a cabbage or eggplant and put a thick candle into the hollow. Surround with leafy kale and smaller votive candles.
Start to collect candle holders: brass, pewter, glass, Mexican tin, wall sconces. Group them all together. Fill a low, wide glass bowl with small shells or black stones. Rest short candles of various heights on them. Place thin tapers (they make them as thin as spaghetti) in a floral oasis so they fan out at various heights. Put arrangement on glass plate (wider than the arrangement). Cover oasis with glitter, or green moss, or a mound of shells. Consider placing a stocky candle in a glass salad bowl. Fill the bowl up around the candle. Float flowers in the water.
• Outdoors, you can float candles in pool, fish pond, kids' wading pool. Use tin pie plate to hold candles in water.
• Place candles on all dining areas. If you're eating at a table, place clusters of candles (low enough to see over) on a corner or at the ends of the table.
• Consider placing one votive candle at each place setting.

• For lap or snack-tray dining, place a votive candle on each setup.

• For buffet dining, place candles on buffet and throughout the area where guests will be eating. Decorate votive candles with galax leaves. Wrap galax leaves around glass candle holders. Secure with twine or hemp.

• For economy, buy votive candles at religious supply shops.

• Never, never use scented candles around food. Let the natural aroma of the food dominate.

• Place candles in all parts of the house. Make every room party-ready by creating a festive, alluring mood with candlelight. Place them in entrance hall, bedroom, bath and kitchen, too. Line your driveway with torches.

• And, lastly but most importantly, keep the flame away from fabric or any other combustible material. Keep your eye on all the candles during the evening.

This chapter will spark your imagination by showing you the many ways you can use a variety of things to create interesting table settings and centerpieces. Use these suggestions to find new ways of making your parties special.

You don't need "good" china; you don't even need plates to set a stunning table. And you don't need a lot of money to spend on flowers—just a sense of adventure—to create centerpieces.

TABLE SETUPS:

The following list of table-setting alternatives presents a sampling of the various types of things you can use to make your party tables stunning, unique, and functional.

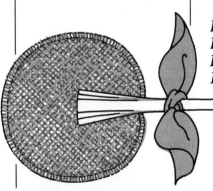

Place mats

Clear glass or lucite squares, edges smoothed
Plain ceramic tiles, 1 inch square; terra cotta, white, pale pastels, red, dark blue, green, or black

Large, printed cotton handkerchiefs
Indian print scarves
Burlap
Bamboo mats
Flat Oriental fans
Plain or quilted cotton place mats
(stay far, far away from plastic mats!)

Wicker trays, 9 by 15 inches, with raised sides
Lacquer trays, 9 by 15 inches, with raised sides
Plywood squares, ¼ inch thick, spray-painted lacquer red or black
Antique runners

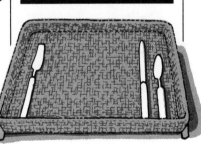

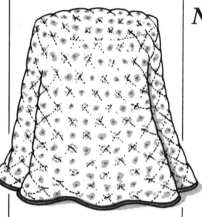

Tablecloths

Printed or solid-
  colored cotton
  sheets
Antique runners,
  sewn together
Quilts
Remnants—satin,
  red China silk,
  cotton prints
Burlap
Grasscloth
Flats of real grass
Paper, black, with
  galax leaves
  smothering it
Crepe paper with
  streamers

Napkins

French linen dish
  towels
Checked Italian
  cotton
Terry-cloth squares
Any plain or printed
  absorbent cotton

Glassware

Any tall, stemmed
  glass for drinks,
  salad, or fruit
Mason jars—
  particularly good
  for Bloody Marys,
  etc.
Glass mugs
A collection of
  completely
  different glasses,
  sizes, shapes

[62]

Dishes

Covered lacquer
    bowls
Clay saucers and
    pots—all sizes,
    with or without
    glass liners
Individual cutting
    boards
Wicker basket, low,
    flat; if unlac-
    quered, lined with
    glass or cotton
    napkin (for certain
    menus)

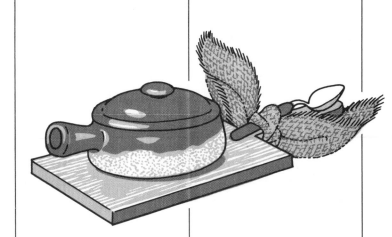

Hobo sacks. Large
    cotton cloth
    holding bread and
    board, literally
Wooden rounds
Large and small
    seashells
Banana leaves and
    tea leaves

Vegetable baskets—
    mushroom, berry
    baskets, with or
    without handles
    for indoor or
    outdoor picnics,
    buffets

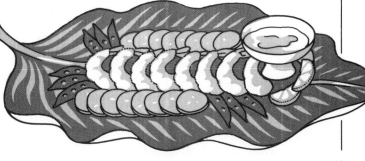

[63]

Condiment Dishes

Molds—for Jell-O, pâté, aspic, etc. Any shape or size for sauces or bread sticks. In short, anything.

Crockery pots from cheese spreads

Jars—from mustard, capers, most anything

Pewter or brass bowls and pitchers

Glasses/goblets for dips

Lucite desk organizers

Glass ashtrays

Pitchers

Clay pots of all sizes. Small for individual butter containers. Larger for dressings, salads, dips, or breadsticks. Make tight by plugging hole with floral clay.

Seashells

Small lacquered boxes—use both top and bottom

Mexican glass and lead jewelry boxes

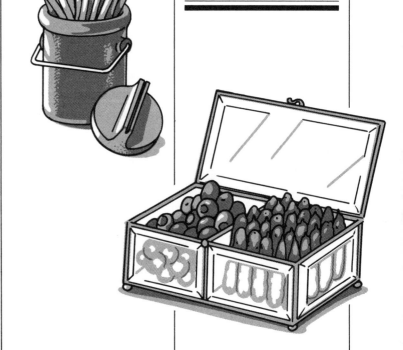

Serving Pieces

Goldfish bowls
Lucite buckets,
  cubes
Large clay pots and
  saucers
Large baskets,
  wicker or raffia
Pumpkins, squash
Wire salad baskets
Three-tiered hanging
  baskets
Stoneware crocks
Old-fashioned gravy
  boats for dips and
  sauces

*I*ce Buckets and
Coolers

> Wheelbarrows
> Barrels and
>   galvanized tubs
> Umbrella stand
> Laundry basket
> Glass bowls
> Punch bowls
> Large clay pot

*C*oasters

> Ceramic tiles
> Glass rounds
> Clay saucers
> Flat fans
> Cork

[66]

TANTALIZING TABLE TOPPINGS

The crowning glory of any table is the centerpiece. It brings beauty and drama to a room. It should be the stage setting for good food, good times, and good conversation. Despite its name, a centerpiece can be off center—to the left, right, or spread all over the table. To create such an arrangement, you need to have a cache of supplies on hand. No matter if you choose to create a look with a bountiful basket of fresh vegetables, flowers and leaves, or ordinary sea-washed pebbles, you need these "tools."

If you have a few of these simple supplies on hand, it will be a lot easier to put together stunning centerpieces. They aren't essential—but they are fun!

From the Florist or Five-and-Ten

Floral clay
Oasis
Frogs
Green florist's wire
Moss

Water vials for single blooms
Green floral tape
Superstick glue

From Hardware Store or Five-and-Ten

T-pins
Styrofoam forms: cylinders, cones, squares
Glitter

Supplies to Collect

Wherever you go, become a nature scavenger. Look for branches, leaves, stones, shells, reeds to use in centerpieces.

Pick up old cups, small vases, oddly shaped containers at garage sales, flea markets, and antique stores. See containers "as if" they were filled with flowers or other natural objects.

Stockpile candles of all shapes and sizes. Votive candles are the least expensive and most versatile.

Collect baskets: from mushroom or fruit containers to wicker, china, and glass.

Look around your house. See what you already have that could make an imaginative vase. Consider this list of possibilities:

Vases

Demitasse cups
mini liqueur bottles
wine glasses
pitchers
fish bowls
canisters
aquariums
mugs

[67]

carafes
bud vases of all sizes
  and shapes
wine bottles
medicine bottles
old perfume bottles
clay pots
glass salad bowls
ice buckets
punch bowls or cups
metal containers
Chinese jars and bases
wood, metal, or
  wicker boxes
all wicker baskets—
  with glass liners
oddly shaped glass
  containers

[68]

How to Put an Arrangement Together

When building an arrangement, you want it to be bold but not overwhelming, grand but not garish. And remember, it should never obstruct sight or conversation across a table.

1. Select container(s) that do not overpower the arrangement. If using large vases or baskets, make arrangement at least 1½ times the height of the vase.

2. When creating an arrangement that is made up of several vases or objects, place them at various heights. Never have all objects aligned top to bottom, right to left, or back to front.

3. Create an arrangement that is appropriate to the mood of the party. Although it is not necessary to have "theme" arrangements, they should carry out the general feel of the party, food, decor, and table settings. A Chinese takeout dinner calls for a centerpiece of either Oriental vegetables, fans, chopsticks, one dramatic flower in a low glass bowl filled with small black rocks, or one large branch of flowering forsythia. A country-brunch arrangement may be made up of fresh fruit, old-fashioned cups and saucers decorated with violets and lilies of the valley, a collection of old cooking implements, or a casual assortment of wild flowers or grasses.

4. Keep arrangements simple and bold. Build an arrangement slowly, starting with the shortest components. Evaluate their placement in terms of line, shape. Add each larger or taller component one at a time. Create visual rhythm by staggering position left to right, top to bottom, and front to back.

5. When using plants, take clues from the way the plants, branches, flowers grow in nature. Imitate their natural growth lines.
Pay attention to how they change after they are cut. Do stems move, curve? Tulips, anemones, and all hollow-stemmed flowers will "move" after being arranged. Stiff, stalked flowers, such as carnations, gladiolas, and mums, will stay put.
More elegant arrangements usually have components that are all one color or subtle shades. Casual arrangements combine more colors in a festive array. (There are, of course, many exceptions to this, but it is a good guideline for a beginning flower arranger.)

6. Edible arrangements can be designed to be consumed, or may simply be there for a visual feast. In either case, keep them fresh by spritzing them with ice water throughout the evening.

7. You may put an arrangement on individual snack or lap trays. In front of each place setting on a table, down the whole length of the table. On a buffet. Or simply on a mantelpiece, bookshelf, or the floor.

[69]

8. Place arrangement so it catches the eye. You can transform an inadequate arrangement into a commanding presence by placing it correctly. Generally speaking, small arrangements should be at desk height or higher. Large arrangements can work on the floor, at table height, or at eye level.

Taking Care of Plants for Arrangements

• Keep heat low and humidity high around plants.
• Add 7-Up or sugar water to roses or tulips to keep them fresh.
• When using heavy branches, hammer the ends before putting in water so they can drink it up.
• Cut all flower stems on an angle before putting in water.

Creating a Finished Look

There are boundless ways to dress up your party table. I have my favorites, and I'd like to show you how I put them together. Using various alternative table settings and inexpensive natural arrangements, you can assert your party style and personality with zest and creativity.

When you read over these examples, notice how the table setting and centerpiece work together to produce a distinctive party look. Try to come up with variations on these setups. Use them as a starting point for creating your own individual look.

Terra-Cotta Table

If you don't have a set of dishes that work for stylish entertaining, consider terra cotta. Those beautiful plant pots and saucers can be used to create an unexpectedly beautiful table.

• *Use 12-inch saucers lined with glass plates for serving and eating.*
• *Use mini saucers for butter dishes.*
• *Dress table with place mats made from leaves.*
• *Create the centerpiece using herb pots. Thyme, basil, chives are all gorgeous. Remember to place pots at various heights to give arrangement rhythm and texture.*
• *Put soft, green Boston lettuce in small clay pots. Drape ivy across table.*
• *Go all-out with this look—don't do it halfway. Turn the table into a bountiful garden.*
• *Keep the feeling going by serving food that is fresh, light, and "country."*

[71]

The Rockery

If you're trying to create drama on your table, you've got the solution in your back yard.

For a minimum outlay of money, you can have a table that is daring but elegantly simple.

- *Bring a large, irregular-faced rock to the table. Decorate it with moss and small daisies. Keep the look spare and Oriental.*
- *Spread flat, smooth black pebbles across the table.*
- *Keep plates and serving pieces simple, using glass or white china.*
- *Knot napkins and rest on plates.*
- *Sprinkle votive candles across table.*

Seashell Buffet

The buffet table is difficult to arrange so that it is both functional and resplendent. My favorite solution is this seashell buffet.

- *Use large shells placed on small bamboo tables for serving pieces. Here, cold pasta and vegetables are attractively displayed.*
- *Mini shells hold salt and pepper.*
- *Bread sticks are arranged in medium-sized shells filled with soft butter.*
- *The long wooden toothpicks for spearing the pasta share space with a candle in a tapered shell.*
- *Arrange this spread on a bare wood table. Keep dishes, napkins, and flatware simple.*

[73]

Hobo Sacks

If you are picnicking indoors or out, the hobo sack makes an elegant, economical package for each diner.

• *Cut 30-inch circles of heavy cotton fabric for each sack.*
• *Lace thick yarn or twine through edge to create drawstring.*
• *Sew in pockets on inside for napkins and silverware.*
• *Place round wooden board on center of cloth. Arrange cheese, fruit, bread, finger food on it. Put in individual-sized wine bottle and glass.*
• *Close sack.*
• *Place one sack by each floor pillow or on picnic cloth spread out on living room floor or outdoors.*
• *Double sacks can be made. Include two napkins and sets of silverware, a second bottle of wine and glass, and a double portion of food.*

Wicker Wilderness

Indoors or out, the look of wicker is always eye-pleasing. The shapes, textures, and colors of the baskets create interest on any table.

• *Use a large basket to hold vegetable crudités. Plant a miniature tomato plant in the basket. Surround with moss or lettuce leaves. Arrange cut vegetables so that shapes and colors form an interesting pattern.*
• *Line low, flat baskets with glass or foil to hold skewered melon and ham, cheese, or other finger foods. On a table, nestle dishes of dips and sauces on beds of lettuce, grass, or plant leaves. Outdoors, rest them on the ground.*
• *Remember—any dish can look more appetizing if you take the time to dress it up. Wicker is one of the cheapest and easiest devices.*

Flower Arrangements

If you choose to use flowers to create your centerpieces or arrangements, there are many ways to provide drama and beauty without breaking your budget.

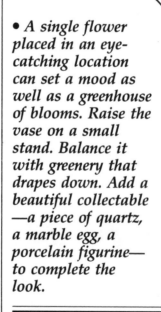

• *A single flower placed in an eye-catching location can set a mood as well as a greenhouse of blooms. Raise the vase on a small stand. Balance it with greenery that drapes down. Add a beautiful collectable —a piece of quartz, a marble egg, a porcelain figurine— to complete the look.*

• *Three large tea or banana leaves in a handsome vase can transform a table or a room. Place oversized vases on tables or mantelpieces for extra drama. Put them on the floor to soften corners or create space divisions.*

• *For a festive country look, you can put together an array from your garden using wild flowers and weeds such as Queen Anne's lace, reeds, branches, or cut flowers. Keep the arrangement loose. Let leggy or branchy stems create a frame around the outside and back of the arrangement. Fill in the center and lower portions with a variety of colors and textures.*

• For a real summer look, use flats of grass as centerpieces. Stud them with short blooms of inexpensive flowers such as daisies. Create height by using two or three tall, firm stalked blooms, like tulips. Put stems in individual glass vials (such as roses come in) and plant in soil.

• An easy, surprising arrangement can be made by studding a watermelon with a few blooming branches of hydrangea or forsythia. The juice of the melon keeps the flowers fresh.

Natty Napkins

The plainest table can be zipped up by a clever napkin design. Try out these simple techniques. You'll be surprised at how easy they are to do and how much they add to a table.

Lilies

- *Lay large, plain cloth napkin on flat surface.*
- *Roll tightly and evenly from corner to corner as shown.*
- *Fold roll in half and place into goblet.*
- *Turn down top edge of each end of napkin to form lily.*

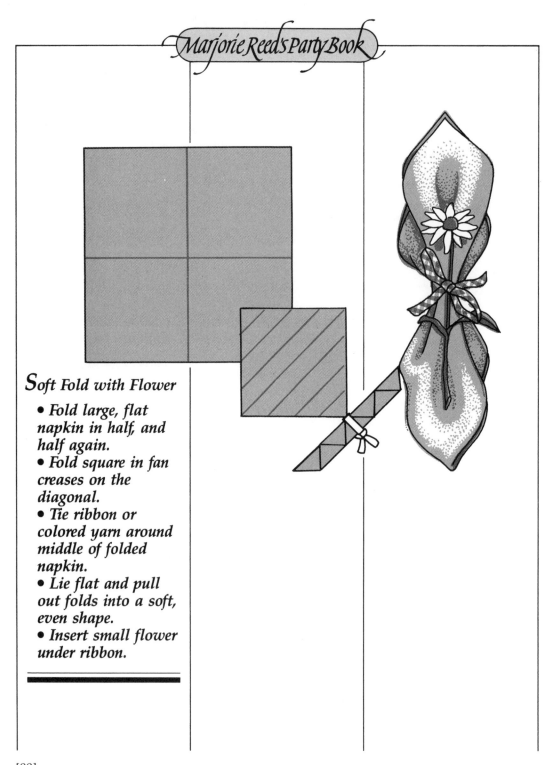

*S*oft Fold with Flower

- *Fold large, flat napkin in half, and half again.*
- *Fold square in fan creases on the diagonal.*
- *Tie ribbon or colored yarn around middle of folded napkin.*
- *Lie flat and pull out folds into a soft, even shape.*
- *Insert small flower under ribbon.*

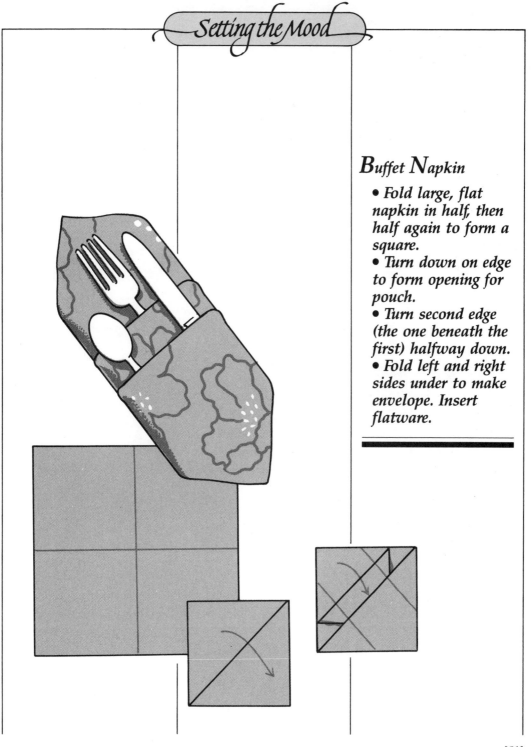

*B*uffet *N*apkin

- *Fold large, flat napkin in half, then half again to form a square.*
- *Turn down on edge to form opening for pouch.*
- *Turn second edge (the one beneath the first) halfway down.*
- *Fold left and right sides under to make envelope. Insert flatware.*

Free Form

- Use a napkin with a scalloped or lacy edge.
- Gather toward center and place in goblet.
- Fan out edges to form loose petals.

CHAPTER •8•

INVITING INVITATIONS

An invitation is your guest's first clue to the spirit of the evening you've planned. It can set the mood and introduce a sense of style with little expense or effort.

So many people forget about the importance of invitations. More and more, we use the phone for all but the most formal of occasions. There are times when phone invitations are the most sensible and appropriate, but I love the special feeling of a mailed invitation. They're a little bit like Christmas cards all year round. They are pretty, surprising, and contain wishes for a happy time.

GENERAL GUIDELINES FOR INVITATIONS

• Issue all invitations on the same day. You can hurt people's feelings if they think they have not been invited. Make all phone calls at the same time. Mail out invitations on the same day.

• When inviting a single person, always let him or her know if he or she can bring a date.

• Don't try to match up singles one for one. There is nothing less natural, or more likely to kill conversation.

• When inviting someone who lives with or has a fairly constant lover, you should include both people. This applies to homosexual as well as heterosexual couples.

• Do not arrange for people to call you back with regrets only. There's too big a margin for error; you never know if someone simply forgot to call or if it means he or she is coming.

• Include the following information in written or phone invitations:

time, including when the party is scheduled to be over if it is for cocktails only.

what kind of party it is, including the amount of food to be served. "We're having people over from seven to ten for cocktails and a light buffet," or "We're having people stop by at eight o'clock after dinner for coffee and dessert."

the occasion—"It's Suzanne's birthday. But please don't bring a present, just your best wishes," or "It's a post-marathon picnic, indoors. Come dressed for jogging."

the attire—this is tricky, so be very specific if it matters to you. Remember, one person's "casual" could be another's "formal." So spell it out. "We're having a few friends for dinner, so just come in your comfortable pants," or "We're having a dinner party. We thought it would be fun to get dressed up for a change. Wear your favorite party dress."

your address and phone number—this, obviously, is a necessity.

INVITATIONS OVER THE PHONE

• Phone invitations work well when you are having a small group of close friends over. They reinforce the feeling of casual intimacy. For enormous bashes, when you don't really care if everyone you invite shows up, you can use the phone, too. However, this creates exactly the opposite effect from issuing phone invitations for a small, intimate evening and makes it seem less personal, less special.

• When issuing an invitation over the phone, *never* expect an immediate acceptance or refusal. "I just wanted to let you know today so you could check your schedule. Call me back in the next couple of days when you know." If someone declines, don't try to change his or her mind!

• Never leave an invitation as a message. Make

sure you speak directly to your guest(s).

• Issue phone invitations ten days to two weeks before the party. This gives guests a few days to call you back without messing up your schedule.

• Sometimes you can issue short-notice phone invitations if you are trying to put together a more spontaneous, relaxed grouping.

• After you have issued the invitations, wait three or four days to see who calls back to accept or refuse. If you have heard from some of the guests by then, you can call others back.

Keep the tone light. "I was just wondering if you were going to be able to join us Tuesday." Don't say, "I will be really disappointed if you can't come." And never say, "Why can't you come?"

Review the invitation. If a guest accepts, repeat the time, address, and nature of party—subtly. "We look forward to seeing you around eight o'clock Friday night for dinner. I know Suzanne will be delighted that you can celebrate her birthday with her. You remember where we're located?"

WRITTEN INVITATIONS

• Written invitations do not have to be reserved for formal occasions only. A hoedown, picnic, dinner party, or evening of dancing and supper merits a written invitation.

• Plan to have your invitations in your guests' hands at least three weeks before the party. This means that you have to allow enough time for the mail to get them there! Unfortunately, this is often hard to predict, so err on the side of extra time.

• If you are planning a real extravaganza and need to have a firm idea

of the final count well ahead of time, allow four weeks. This is particularly important around the holidays, when people's calendars get crowded.

• I always send myself an invitation, too, so I can judge when my guests received theirs!

• If you have not gotten a reply from your guests after four or five days, you may begin making follow-up calls.

• Don't assume that your guests have received the invitations. It is possible that they went astray in the mail. "I'm calling to see if you received the invitation I sent you. We're having people over for dinner on the thirteenth. Why don't you get back to me later today and let me know?" If they haven't received the invitation, they'll question you about the evening, and you can fill them in on details about time, dress, and type of party.

• The burden for understanding is all yours.

Accept it with good grace. Don't say, "You should have let me know sooner."

WRITTEN FOLLOW-UPS

For really formal occasions or grand celebrations, you can follow up written and phone invitations with a short note about ten days before the party.

• Send the note to those guests who have not yet responded with acceptances or regrets. Don't send it to those who have let you know they're not coming.

• Send the note to those who have accepted— just to remind them.

• The note should be very short and light. "I look forward to seeing you Thursday the thirteenth about nine p.m." Sign your name and phone number. That is a subtle encouragement to those who have not yet responded.

CANCELLATIONS

It's a big emotional letdown if you've planned a grand evening and last-minute cancellations threaten to ruin it. Don't hesitate to "fill in" with last-minute invitations.

INNOVATIVE INVITATIONS

The old image of a printed invitation just doesn't apply to the new, creative, individualistic party style. Even the more casual packaged invitations available at paper supply stores lack the cleverness and impact that you want to convey.

I favor self-made cards that are designed to make a definite statement about the special nature of your party. You don't need to be terribly artistic to create your own invitations. Let's look at the kind of impact you can produce with a few simple supplies and a sense of flair.

General Guidelines

• Make the look of the invitation fit the spirit of the party. Before you make up the invitations, think about the look you are going for. Try to imagine the table settings, the centerpieces, the food, and the general decorative touches you are going to use. You don't have to be absolutely definite about these things, but a general idea of the look and feel of the occasion should inform your decision about the type of invitation you mail out.

• Keep your eyes open for clever invitations. Look for postcards, scenics, art reproductions that you like. A snowy picture of the Rockies would make a great invitation to a "Cool Off in the Pool" party during the hot summer months. A reproduction of Manet's "Luncheon on the Grass" would be a delight for announcing a fancy spring brunch or an indoor winter picnic.

For theme parties, look for small, native artifacts. If you're giving a cocktail party with an Oriental flavor—saki or plum wine to drink; sushi, spareribs, and egg rolls for hors d'oeuvres—send out invitations on solid-colored Oriental fans. For an Italian party, write the invitations (with a Magic Marker) on a checkered cotton napkin.

You never know when such items will be handy, so buy them when you spot them and keep available for future parties.

• If you have neither the time nor the inclination to do something elaborate, keep invitations simple and dramatic.

For formal and festive invitations, write information with black or red Magic Marker on a heavy white card stock. Put dots of glue in corners of card and sprinkle silver glitter over them. Or add gold or silver party stickers, which can be bought at any five-and-ten.

For casual occasions, write out invitations with several colorful Magic Markers on the white card stock. Add a pressed flower, a dash of confetti, or a pretty party favor to the envelope.

• Remember, invitations don't have to be sent in small, flat envelopes. You can send them out in boxes, oversized folders, homemade packages, egg cartons, or tennis-ball cans!

Creative Alternatives

Celebrity Match-Up

• Collect postcards of famous couples—Gable and Lombard, Adam and Eve, Fay Wray and King Kong. Each guest gets his/her own invitation—each person in a couple receives his or her own. Guests are to bring the invitations with them to the party. Seating is arranged by "coupling" matched celebrities. The first dance is for these famous pairs. This scheme helps break up paired-off guests, generates conversation between people who don't know one another.

Make sure you explain the idea on the invitation so guests will know what's planned.

Summer in January

• To banish the winter blues, throw a summer party in midwinter. Send Xeroxes of banner headlines from last summer's heat wave *or* enticing travel brochures (available free) with party information on the inside.

After-dinner Dessert Party

• *Send an oversized, homemade chocolate chip cookie nestled in a small box. Decorate with an announcement of your dessert party. Send a bundle of hard candies or foil-wrapped chocolates with invitation card attached.*

Sports party

• For post-tennis, jogging, marathon, or racquet ball parties, send white T-shirts with invitation written in Magic Marker on front. *Note*: When writing on shirt, place an impermeable sheet of foil or heavy cardboard between back and front or else the ink will bleed through.

Fancy Festive Gatherings

• *Make an invitation with a shiny silver Mylar cover. Pen information on an insert of white paper. Decorate the cover with a spray of delicate dried leaves or flowers. Assemble the card by binding the cover and insert together with an elastic silver string. Mail invitation in a box lined with tissue paper.*

Fan Dance

• *Print invitation to a dance in a fine-tip Magic Marker on a plain folding fan. Mail in a small manila envelope. Add streamers or confetti to package.*

CHAPTER •9•

PARTY COUNT DOWN

*T*he best part of planning a party is the fantasy, the daydreaming. In the quiet of your bedroom or the tub, you can let your imagination wander. You can see the way you'll rearrange the living room, smell the subtle aroma of the food, touch the intriguing textures in the centerpieces. In your imagination, you have pulled off a major entertaining success. Throwing a party begins to seem easy. You believe in your entertaining abilities. You feel impulsive!

Terrific. But it's time to slow down. Even the most creative host needs a firm sense of organization. There are some rare people who can carry around their plans in their head. I'm not one of them. There's no pleasure in remembering I wanted to buy two more bags of ice—*after* the party has started. So I make lists, schedules, sketches (very rough!). I plan, ponder, and plan some more. I figure it's the best way to make sure I am confident and cool when the doorbell rings.

LISTS, LISTS, LISTS

The Budget

The very first list is the budget. Before you can decide on the menu, the number of guests, the centerpieces, or the basic type of party, you have to know how much you can spend.

Once you have a rough idea, you can make some preliminary choices:

• A few people—with high per-guest cost—versus many with low per-guest cost.
• Alternative party formats, such as a midday brunch, a picnic, or a bring-your-own casserole, versus a standard cocktail or dinner party.
• Full dinner menu versus pre-dinner hors d'oeuvres or after-din-

ner sweets and munchies.

When planning a budget, always leave a margin for the unexpected. Food is not your only expense; you may have to buy paper goods, rent chairs, or accommodate a last-minute guest.

The Guest List

Once you have a rough idea of your budget, you can decide how many guests you are going to invite. As indicated above, the number can vary greatly depending on the type of party and the amount of food to be served.

The guest list is the most crucial decision you have to make. The careful blending of personalities and interests is the key to a successful, enjoyable evening. You want listeners and talkers, young and old, familiar and new.

Don't's

Don't invite a lot of guests who work together.

Don't invite exactly the same number of men and women. You're not running a dating service.

Don't ask the same people over and over.

Don't ask everyone who is the same age.

Do's

Do ask at least two "new" people to every party. People you've just met and would like to know better. Friends of your friends. Extend your network. Add a new element, a surprise personality.

Do ask as many single men or women as you like.

Do try to keep in mind the work and other interests of guests. Avoid asking a nuclear engineer and an antinuke activist to the same small dinner party unless you like to have a reputation for controversial evenings (not necessarily a bad thing).

Do ask as many people as you can possibly handle. Remember, at a large party of seventy-five or more, a 66 percent turn-out is considered standard.

Do fill in last-minute cancellations. If you have asked eight dinner guests and two cancel, it can look like a sparse gathering. Call another couple (be frank), even if it's at the last minute. Tell them, "We are having a small group over for dinner. The guest list keeps fluctuating. I'm sorry to get to you so late, but we'd love to have you join us if you're free."

The Menu

Planning a menu takes many of the same abilities as putting together a guest list. You must have a sense of how things go together; what contrasts are provocative and pleasing, what looks good together; what tastes can be combined.

Eating should be a sensual experience. Food stimulates us through its aroma, texture, taste, and even sound if it sizzles or pops. Let yourself enjoy its tantalizing qualities. This will help you put together intriguing, pleasing menus.

When you think about putting together a party menu, follow these basic guidelines:

• Serve any one type of food only once in the course of a meal. Don't offer guests cheese as an appetizer, cheese sauce on the broccoli at dinner, and cheesecake for dessert.

• Generally, serve only one dish per meal that is prepared with a sauce. If you have a hot and creamy coquilles St. Jacques for a first course, don't offer Hungarian chicken with sour cream and paprika for the entrée.

• Menus are usually built from the lightest to the heaviest foods. Obviously, lamb kebabs as hors d'oeuvres will overpower fillet of sole as an entrée.

• Put food together that has different colors. Chicken, white rice, and cauliflower make for a pale and unattractive plate. But a chicken cutlet garnished with thin strips of lemon peel and combined with the vivid green of a spinach purée and the delicate orange of glazed baby carrots is very enticing.

• Combine food with different textures. Crunchy with smooth, chewy with soft, fried with steamed, leafy with grainy. In a salad, combine leafy romaine or endive with a variety of ingredients: a semi-soft cheese such as blue or feta, bacon bits, water chestnuts, olives, mandarin oranges, sliced turkey. Various combinations produce a real flavor and texture. Soft fish, puréed vegetables, and mashed potatoes make a meal the texture of baby food!

• Combine bold flavors—but with a gentle hand. If you are serving Mexican, Thai, Szechuan, or Indian food, you can combine sweet ingredients with a wide variety of spicy flavors that complement one another. But unless those seasonings are combined purposefully, they will simply cancel each other out and leave your guests with little feeling for the special quality of each dish.

• Avoid any food that has an overpowering smell. You want to be able to appreciate the aroma of each dish. A dining room full of the smell of eau de cabbage is not what you're aiming for.

• Make the menu fit the spirit of the evening. You can give a picnic on the floor and serve nothing but finger food *or* an amazingly gourmet smorgasbord; *but* each creates a different mood, feeling, for the evening. Know what you are trying to create. This is as true for a cocktail hors d'oeuvres tray as for a seated dinner. Think about the connotations of certain foods. Use them or play against them.

• Know your guests' eccentricities and tastes. If you don't, inquire. Guests who are vegetarian, on restricted diets, or just plain finicky should (voluntarily) let the host know, but often are reluctant to broach the subject.

Putting the Menu Together

• No matter what kind of party you are throwing, there are some simple techniques that will spare your nerves and save time.

Cook only one complicated dish per meal, and then only if you insist. Make it something that can be prepared in advance.

Never serve anything that takes last-minute preparation. You shouldn't be spending your time in the kitchen when your guests arrive.

Hot food should be served *hot*—not lukewarm. If you can't keep it hot, don't serve it. The reverse is true for cold food.

Plan on serving at least two cold courses in any meal, or have at least two out of three appetizers served cold.

Have a durable entrée. You never know when guests will run late or pre-dinner conversation will become too enjoyable to interrupt. Have food that can stay warm in the kitchen without being ruined.

Choose food that you have the right serving piece for. Also, make sure it looks good on your dishes. You want your food to be attractively presented and easy to serve.

Avoid "controversial" foods as a main course. Many people don't like organ meats, snails, hot, spiced food, etc. If you do serve them, offer an alternative, too.

Never plan to cook a dish for the first time. Always try out a new recipe the week before the party. You never know what surprises may be in store for you.

The Shopping List

When you write out your shopping list, include:

• Specific ingredients for each recipe.

• Garnishes for each dish; greens; extra tomatoes for color; lemon, lime, or carrots for grating; anything that catches your eye.

• Supplies for bar.

• Paper goods.

• Backups—"just in case," and to avoid the "oh, my's." An extra package of rolls—just in case they burn. An extra box of crackers—in case everyone eats more appetizers than you planned on.

• Be flexible! You may have decided to serve asparagus. But when you get to the store, it's five times more expensive than broccoli. Your budget doesn't need asparagus, and frankly, neither do your guests. When you come right down to it, your final choices should be based on freshness, appearance, and price.

Shopping tips

• Shop early. Stock the shelves. If you know that you like to make ratatouille, buy tomato paste or whole, canned tomatoes when they are on sale. Save for a party. Once you've set the menu, be on the lookout for bargains.

• Cook once, serve

twice. Buy in quantity when making sauces, stews, and other "freezable" foods.

• Avoid prepared foods. It is rarely cheaper to buy a ready-made appetizer or vegetable soufflé, and these items certainly lack the flavor, color, nutrition, and aroma of the fresh.

• Never shop when you're hungry! It is fatal to the budget.

• Look for wholesale or discount outlets for vegetables, flowers, and glasses. Read through the yellow pages. Look up local distributors, warehouses. Call. You'll be surprised at the bargains you can uncover.

• If you need to shop for serving pieces or dishes, comb garage sales and thrift and antique shops. You can often find some wonderful old platters, pitchers, dessert saucers, and the like.

Decorations List

Once you've determined your menu, you want to decide how you're going to decorate the table and the house.

• Do you need candles? What sizes, colors? How many? Candle holders? Can you make some? Vases? Baskets? Holders for flowers or centerpieces? Styrofoam bases for centerpieces?

• Roughly sketch out your centerpiece. List its ingredients.

• If you need fresh flowers or fruit and vegetables for a centerpiece, try to arrange with the florist or vegetable store to have them on hand. Let the store know what you will need and what day you'll need it (the day before the party). That way, you can be relatively sure your centerpiece and decorating ideas will not fall through.

• Take inventory of seating. Do you need pillows for the floor or the bed? Do you need a bedcover, or new slipcovers for chairs?

• Do you need a special table covering, a remnant of silk fabric, burlap, printed cotton?

• What special touches are you going to make in your house? A variety of low tables scattered on the floor to hold food or drinks? Several oversized wicker baskets to hold long loaves of French bread or spring's first wisteria branches? A movable screen to divide the kitchen from the dining area? A kerosene lamp on the mantelpiece? Concentrate on seeing the house "as if" it were already party-ready. What do you see?

• Put your money into reusable investments. Go for basics in glass, wicker, lacquer, and for solid colors in fabrics that can be combined with different looks over and over again. Let the flowers or centerpiece be the one "perishable" extravagance.

COUNTDOWN AGENDA

This is a basic outline of the timing for getting your party together with minimum panic. Play with the schedule. Discover what routine works for you. Once you find what you are comfortable with, make a countdown agenda

[93]

whenever you entertain. Don't cut corners here. Take the time to think through and write down every step in the process.

THREE TO FOUR WEEKS TILL PARTY DAY

Set budget.

Determine size and type of party.

Set guest list.

Issue written invitations.

Four weeks before party day—send written invitations to special event or holiday parties.

Three weeks before party day—send written invitations to "standard" entertainment.

TWO WEEKS TILL PARTY DAY

Issue phone invitations.

Set menu, read cookbooks, look through magazines.

Write out menu and post it on your refrigerator door.

Live with it for a couple of days. Think about the preparation time and effort, the taste compatibility, the presentation.

Write out list of table settings, bar setup, and centerpieces. Sketch setup. Plan buffets for traffic flow. Try out table setting to make sure it is not too crowded or cluttered.

Plan where you will set up bar, appetizers, buffet, dining table, dessert service.

Write out list of serving pieces needed. For appetizers, each course, drinks, dessert. Include serving utensils, salt and pepper, butter dishes, condiment bowls.

Compare lists for menu, table setting, and serving pieces. Do they seem compatible? Do you need to change the menu to accommodate the look of the food that you want? Or to make more room at each place setting? Do you have the serving pieces you need?

Finalize menu. Test out any untried recipes. Adjust menu if needed after that.

ONE WEEK TILL PARTY DAY

Day Seven: Begin shopping for nonperishable food. Call guests who have not R.S.V.P.'ed to finalize guest list.

Assemble your party clothes. Check to make sure everything is clean and pressed. Select accessories, stockings, shoes. Place all accessories together in a Baggie and hang with clothes in closet so everything is together when you go to get dressed. Your party clothes should be comfortable, but festive. Avoid anything with long, flowing sleeves or tight skirts. You want to be able to get around easily without dragging your sleeves through food or knocking over glasses. The host should always be slightly more dressed up than the guests. THIS SETS A FESTIVE TONE. Make sure you choose colors that blend with the decor—all white is a perfect solution. Consider slacks with a tunic top, or floor-length caftan. Ethnic dressing sets a festive mood, too. Whatever you choose, make sure it makes you feel pretty and confident.

Day Six: Arrange with liquor store, vegetable man, and butcher for items you will need later in the week. Go over house, assessing what you need for seating, ashtrays, coasters, lighting, and so forth. Get what's missing.

Day Five: Go through serving pieces. Arrange them in cupboards so you can get to them when you need to. Make sure nothing is missing or cracked. Check place settings. Make name cards; write out seating chart.

Day Four: Begin housecleaning. Pay attention to every room, each corner. Decide on your attire for party. Make sure you've got what you need, that everything is fresh and clean. If you

are making ice—not buying it—start now.

Day Three: If serving fruit, buy it today so it can ripen. Begin cooking. Certain menu items can be prepared in advance. Your menu should contain at least two such dishes. Continue getting house ready.

Day Two: Buy all perishable foods, vegetables, greens, fish. Have liquor and flowers delivered. Chill beverages. Let flower buds open so they are fully bloomed tomorrow. Set up floral arrangements. Edible centerpieces cannot be done ahead of time. Put finishing touches on house. Stock bathroom with necessities for guests—needle and thread, perfume, comb and brush. Put in a big wicker basket with a sign: "Help yourself!"

Day One: Morning: Set up table, buffet, and bar with basic supplies, dishes. Rearrange furniture as needed. Set out candles, ashtrays, coasters, cocktail napkins.

Read through menu and shopping lists—taped on the refrigerator door. Make sure you haven't forgotten the whipped cream for dessert or the watercress for a garnish. Give house its last touch-up. Sit down. Read. Take a deep breath.

Afternoon: Finish cooking and assembling food. Time the cooking, reheating, and assembly of food so that you can eat about an hour after guests arrive. If serving hors d'oeuvres, they should be out and ready to eat as guests arrive. If serving hot hors d'oeuvres, time them so the first batch is ready about fifteen minutes after the guests' scheduled arrival. (Always have cold munchies around to fill in during that time gap.) Finalize centerpieces and arrangements. Keep in refrigerator if possible, in parts or whole. If using leafy vegetables, have a water sprayer handy to perk them up after they have been assembled. Use ice-cold water.

[95]

Spritz—inconspicuously —during the evening.

Two hours before the party: Draw a hot tub. Pour yourself a glass of sherry. Soak for twenty minutes. Meditate. Do deep breathing. Concentrate on "as if" spirit. Imagine the party as if it were going on—perfectly. Walk from room to room in your mind. Survey scene. Concentrate on details. See what you have put into your rooms that you may have forgotten in reality. Now's the time to feel as good about yourself as possible. Reinforce your confidence. Take pride in the planning and organization you've done.

Ninety minutes before the party: Get dressed, do hair, make up—at least preliminarily. If you leave yourself for last, you will not have enough time to feel your best.

One hour before the party: Back into kitchen. Check on food. Walk through entire house. Look for last-minute touch-ups.

Walk through the traffic pattern. Think about your guests, who they are, what their interests are, what you want to talk to them about, whom you want to introduce to whom.

Last Minute: Put out ice, chilled wines. Open red wine to breathe. Put ice mold into punch bowl. Remember the first steps you will go through when your guests begin to arrive: greeting them; taking coats; making introductions; getting drinks and offering food; guiding the grouping of people; watching for the isolated guest, a potential argument.

PARTY DYNAMICS: TEN STEPS TO A SUCCESSFUL PARTY

Getting ready to throw a party is half the battle; actually getting through the evening is the other half. This simple party dynamics checklist will give you a

good idea of what has to be done—and how to do it. Being a host means having to be in four places at once while appearing to stand calmly in one place. It means being a greeter, a seater, a cook, a bartender, a conversationalist, a temper-smoother, an ashtray-dumper, and an all-around backstage orchestrator. But you know that. And that's what makes it all so nerve-racking.

Step One : The Front Door

The area around the front door should be as uncongested as possible. Have a place for coats and boots that is well out of the way. If possible, provide a mirror at the entrance so guests can freshen up before entering the party. Make sure lighting is adequate, but not glaring.

Step Two: Saying Hello

When a group of guests arrives, you need to greet them, take their coats and any gifts, flowers, or wine they may have brought, and make them feel instantly at home.

If guests who don't know each other arrive at the same time, introduce them after you've put away their coats. It can be awkward to try to do everything at once.

If people bring flowers, don't feel you have to put them in a vase instantly. They will survive for a while. Don't distract yourself from the more important job of greeting guests and making introductions.

If a guest brings a date whom you don't know, introduce yourself immediately. "Hi, I'm Marjorie. I'm so glad Dasha could bring you with her tonight." Make the "stranger" feel like a welcome friend.

Once the party has begun to roll, you still must greet each arriving guest. Don't let another guest open the door for you. Keep your ear tuned for the doorbell and excuse yourself from conversation whenever it rings.

Step Three: Bringing Guests into the Party

After greeting guests, you want to bring them into the party. Don't ever wave your hand in the general direction of the bar or crowd and say: "Make yourself at home." Most people freeze in their tracks. Instead, walk with them.

Step Four: Introductions

In a small or a large party, take the time to introduce each person. Always use both first and last names.

In a *small group*, you can make a general introduction, saying: "I'd like you to meet Suzanne Greene and Jay Ford. This is Robert and Mary Rubin, Sally Jones, Sandra Black, and Jordan Smith. Suzanne is the woman I'm always telling you about. She does those amazing needlepoints. Jay is a friend of my sister. They work together at the bank."

After you make such a general introduction, take the two new guests away from the group. "Come with me. Let's get you a drink before you sit down."

Then walk them back to the group. You should have an idea about whom they will hit it off with. Bring them over to meet that person. "Sandra, I've been wanting to introduce you to Suzanne and Jay. They both have incredible luck with indoor, flowering plants. I know you have quite a collection of African violets. I bet you can trade secrets."

In a *large party*, take arriving guests to the bar first. Then, if other guests are arriving, you can excuse yourself for a moment, greet those guests, bring them to the bar, and rejoin the first couple. Walk them into the crowd and introduce them to specific people. If you can, mention something about their interests. Light a spark so they can get a conversation started.

In a large party, you should repeat this process throughout the evening. "Sally, come with me. I've been dying to introduce you to my friend Jordan."

Keep the group mixing by continuing to orchestrate the combinations of people and the conversation.

Have an eye out at all times for "quiet spots," or

guests who look like they may have been trapped too long with the same person.

The success of a party depends almost entirely on your attention to introductions and your continual mixing of people.

Step Five: Cultivating the "Third Eye"

Once all guests have arrived, you will have to begin to oversee the general course of the evening. While your attention is focused on a particular conversation, you want to keep tabs on what's going on in every corner. Adopt a checklist:

- Are ashtrays too full?
- Have candles burned down too far, or are they dripping?
- Does the bar need more ice, sodas, wine, or liquor?
- Have people been helping themselves to hors d'oeuvres?
- Do guests need refills of drinks?
- Is there a glass without a coaster on a good wood table?

- Do the lights need to be dimmed?

Make attention to such details second nature. Take care of them subtly and quietly. Don't look around distractedly. Cultivate a slow, unanxious way of appraising the party environment.

Step Six: Spotting Trouble

Sometimes an argument flares up between guests. It is your job to moderate it. If it is a discussion about a specific topic, and all involved seem to enjoy the heated exchange, let it continue. But if you sense hostility developing, intervene gently. "I really hate to interrupt you, but I need Freddie's help opening the wine. You'll just have to call a temporary halt."

If it cannot be easily defused, be blunt but friendly. "Come on, the rest of us would also like to have a chance to talk with you. You two are getting too heated up! Come over here and tell us about your new boat. I understand it's a real beauty."

With a guest who has drunk too much, be gentle but firm. "John, I am delighted that you were able to come tonight. And I look forward to having you over again, but right now you are not at your best. I know you don't want to embarrass yourself. I've called you a cab. Let's get your coat."

Sometimes, however, this approach won't work. Then it is better to take the guest away from the main party area. Bring him coffee and make him lie down. He'll be glad for the peace and quiet. If all else fails, don't hesitate to get tough. Ask a friend of the problem guest for help. Escort the guest out and have him driven home. In the worst situation, it might be better to ask your guests to leave.

Whatever you do, don't let a rowdy drunk dominate your party. This will kill conversation and make everyone uncomfortable. The temporary scene caused by your intervention will be forgotten when the drunken guest departs. But the discomfort and problems caused by a "hands-off" approach will pollute the whole evening.

Step Seven: Keeping Yourself Fresh

Once you have gotten the party going, you can excuse yourself for a couple of minutes. Retreat to the bathroom. Comb your hair. Enjoy a moment's quiet. Splash on some refreshing cologne. Check your appearance. You'll feel a lot better if you know you aren't frazzled-looking!

Step Eight: Checking the Kitchen

If you are giving a lunch, brunch, or dinner party, you will need to tend to the food while your guests are conversing over appetizers and drinks. The first course should be served cold so it can be put out before guests are seated. Main-course food should be kept warm in the oven or stove top. The salad should be dished up ahead of time on individual plates and put in the refrigerator. Dressing can be poured on at the last minute. Bread and condiments should already be on the table. Don't disappear into the kitchen for too long. You don't want to impress your guests with your drudgery.

Step Nine: Dinner Is Served

It is time to eat about an hour after the guests have arrived. Have your spouse or best friend begin the procession to the table (or buffet). It is hard to get a group moving until someone has made the first move. Don't be too pushy or insistent. And don't interrupt the flow of good conversation. Be flexible.

You should always know where you want your guests to sit, no matter if you are dining at a table or eating off lap trays or snack tables.

The first course should be at each place when guests are seated. Once it is finished by everyone, it should be cleared off quickly. If you are assembling main-course plates in the kitchen, enlist a helper to serve them. If food is to be dished up at the table, make sure that task can be done easily, in individually sized portions. For dinners of more than six, place two small bowls of each side dish and condiment at either end of the table so food doesn't have to be passed all the way around.

Once the main course is finished, you can wait a few minutes to clear the table. Let guests languish, digest, and savor the flavors and conversation. When you do clear, do it as quickly as possible.

Coffee should be prepared ahead of time. Cups and saucers, cream and sugar, should be set out on a counter or tea cart. It is best to pour coffee from your seat and pass the cups around the table. Cream and sugar should be at both ends of the table.

If you are going to have dessert at the table, you may want to mix up the group by having them change seats. Plan out your secondary seating chart ahead of time. "Evelyn, I'd like you and Leonard to change seats. Anne, you change with William." Do it slowly, two

Perhaps you'd like to print names on small, folding fans spread open behind each plate, or to combine name cards with shells, a stack of poker chips, or a mini eggplant.

For festive occasions, take wide, silvery ribbon, cut it into a V, and drape it over each plate. Use press-on letters in silver, black, or white to identify each person's place.

For buffets, when your guests are seated on chairs and sofas or on the floor, attach a balloon with name written in Magic Marker to the back of the guest's seat.

at a time.

You may wish to serve dessert in the living room.

Coffee, liqueurs, and dessert can be served from a coffee table. Make sure guests have trays or tables to rest cups, glasses, and plates on. Have dessert, drinks, and coffee set up on large platters or trays so they can be carried out easily.

Step Ten: Winding Down

After dinner, the music should be soft, the lighting subdued, and the conversation easy. Let people relax over coffee and dessert. If serving it in the living room, you will want to clear off dirty plates and cups, leaving only after-dinner drink glasses.

If guests are enjoying themselves, they may overstay their welcome. This does happen, but it isn't a compliment to have them stay too long. You are weary and ready to kick off your shoes. But still they persist. If you are stuck with one or two hangers-on, there are several gentle ways to hint that the party's over.

"Would you like a last cup of coffee?"

"This has been a wonderful evening. I'm so glad we got a chance to really visit with you. We'll have to do it again soon."

Or, if all else fails: "I hate to collapse on you, but I'm really exhausted. It's been marvelous, but all good things must end."

Don't let yourself be held hostage in your own home!

Name Cards

Name cards are both practical and attractive. You don't have to use those stiff, formal-looking cards that appear in most books on entertaining. You want every part of your table to contribute to the special look of the evening.

Name cards are an attractive and useful device. They free you to clear away drink glasses and appetizers from the living room while your guests seat themselves. (If you don't use name cards, you will need to seat your guests personally. Therefore, it is helpful to have a couple of large trays in the living room to put glasses and appetizer plates on

just before you begin serving the main course. You can carry them to the kitchen quickly after dinner.)

Whether you have used name cards or are directing the seating personally, you will need to write out a

Consider painting guests' names on shiny black stones.
Or serve half bottles of wine at each place setting. Write guests' names on the labels.

seating chart if you have more than six for dinner. A seating chart keeps you from having to shuffle everyone around, and assures that you will not make seating errors.

There are two schools of thought about seating guests:

One: that couples should never be seated together. This attitude protects against couples talking only to one another and prevents the possibility of public discussion of private matters if a couple do not happen to be getting along.

Two: that it is more comfortable if couples sit together. It makes people more at ease to be near someone they know well. Conversation is more easily generated between people when there is a built-in backup.

Personally, I feel it depends on the overall group. If there are several couples who do not know one another, it is helpful to keep them close together. In a group where everyone is friends, seating can be looser.

I do think, however, that these guidelines are helpful:

Don't seat people boy-girl, boy-girl. The effect is that of a high-school mixer and implies that guests should not be single.

Always consider the interests and occupations of guests. You should know enough about them to plan conversation sparkers: "Jenny, I've seated you next to Robert because I know he'd love to hear about your trip to Mexico." You plant the idea for the first topic of conversation. This allows you to continue your role as subtle mixer.

Don't separate people of different ages. It's insulting to them. Mix ages and you'll increase everyone's enjoyment.

AFTER THE PARTY'S OVER

It's hard to know why it's such a letdown when the last guest leaves. I suspect the reason is a combination of exhaustion, a dread of cleanup, and a feeling of anticlimax. To help get over post-party depression, it helps if the cleanup, at least, is not too overwhelming a task.

The following tips may help you wind down easily.

Prepare large garbage containers before the party starts. Have them lined with plastic bags. During the course of the evening, keep dumping ashtrays, throwing away paper goods, cleaning off plates and dishes. Throw as you go.

Set trays out around drinking and eating areas so you can clear glasses and plates efficiently and inconspicuously.

Set up soaking tubs for dishes and glasses. Keep them out of the way—in the sink or oven, or under kitchen counters or tables. If you don't have a dishwasher, let dishes soak. When it's time to wash, it'll be easy.

Have plenty of refrigerator containers available for storing leftovers. Transfer food from serving pieces to storage containers immediately after clearing table. Stash in the fridge and soak the pans. Don't stack up bowls and pans half filled with food. It will look as if pandemonium has set in and there's more chaos than necessary.

Rearrange furniture when guests leave, but *first* notice if they've moved it around to make it more functional. Take a hint from the spontaneous changes that were made. Try to learn what works.

Don't feel you have to clean everything up. Get things in shape so you won't be depressed in the morning. Then pour yourself a drink, sit back, and rerun the tapes! Praise yourself for your success and enjoy the memory of another achievement in entertaining.

CHAPTER •10•

THE CLEVER COOK

*T*he house is in order, the invitations sent. You've thought up some wonderful new ways to set the table and use the house. Now it's time to get down to determining your menu . . . and cooking it.

Cooking can often be the most intimidating part of party planning. So often we feel we have to outdo, outspend, outcook each other. So much of our party gets tied up in what we cook. We stretch our culinary skills to their limit, trying daring new recipes for the first time (a big mistake). Budgets collapse. Soufflés fall. Nerves fray.

None of this is necessary.

The purpose of this chapter is to serve not as a cookbook, but as a guide to help you simplify the task of party cooking. You will learn how to ease your anxiety by using shortcuts and clever cooking techniques.

We all want our party menu to be beautiful to look at and to taste. But few of us have the time, money, or inclination to spend a week in the kitchen. Luckily, to achieve good-tasting, elegant, well-presented menus, we don't have to do that!

I'm no cook. Honestly. And I don't really want to become a great chef. I'm more interested in spending time relaxing with my guests than fussing in the kitchen. I want to use every shortcut possible. But I love food—its flavor, colors, the sensuality of its smell and texture. So I have discovered a way to create elegant menus that are simple and economical. I call it the "Jazz-It-Up Technique."

WHAT IS THE JAZZ-IT-UP TECHNIQUE?

Jazz-It-Up cooking saves you time and money without sacrificing elegance or flavor in party menus.

All dishes are simple,

easy to cook. Special zip is provided by elementary additions of garnishes, flavorings, and flavor boosters.

Food is brought to the table in a stunning presentation. Time is spent making each platter, bowl, and condiment dish look like a work of art. Even simple fare is transformed by the way it is "dressed up."

To demonstrate how you can use the Jazz-It-Up Technique, I have selected six Budgeted Menus, three for a dinner party and three for a cocktail party. There is also a "takeout" menu. Each is followed by a selection entitled Putting Your Best Food Forward. Here you will see how you can transform ordinary dishes into special treats by mastering the art of food presentation. Finally, there is a section called Off the Shelf. Tasty, unusual, and eye-catching party food can be created "instantly" when you keep your shelves stocked with a few versatile items. If you can't cook, don't have the time, or need to throw together a festive meal at the last minute, Off the Shelf will be your best friend.

GUIDE TO CULINARY CLEVERNESS

In order to become a relaxed, confident cook, you must be able to make friends with food! To think of it as a wonderful world of possibilities—not as a mysterious substance in a dangerous laboratory!

• Stimulate your culinary imagination. Think of food as a sensual experience. Tune in to its taste, texture, color, aroma, and shape.
• Look at food in stores, magazines, and cookbooks as if it were a palette for your palate. You want to paint a taste treat.
• Learn to identify garnishes that will perk up the look of food. When you see a bin of oranges, don't just think of orange juice; think of the delicate aroma and flavor of the grated rind, the bright splash of color it can contribute to a chicken salad or to a scoop of vanilla ice cream. Imagine a mound of oranges studded with cloves and

highlighted with sprigs of greenery as a centerpiece for brunch.
• Read through cookbooks, but don't take the recipes too literally. Learn basic cooking techniques. And remember, very few recipes will fail if you substitute basil for thyme, chicken for veal. Let cookbooks serve as a springboard for your imagination.
• Accept your culinary limitations. If omelets or fried chicken are your only skills, stick to them. But apply Jazz-It-Up Techniques to make them suitable party food.
• Taste, taste, taste! Expose yourself to as many different food experiences as possible. Learn to savor food. When it is served to you, observe its arrangement on a plate. Breath in its aroma. Touch it. Learn to read its freshness and quality. And when you prepare something, taste it continually. Evaluate it as you are cooking. Don't ever take anything to the table that you haven't sampled.

THE MENUS

Let's look at the Budgeted Menus now. They should serve as general guides for the types of meals you can turn into successful party fare. Get a feel for the combinations of food used. Don't hesitate to substitute your favorite soup for the one suggested in the first menu. Or to make alterations in flavorings. The menus and their presentations should help you develop confidence in your entertaining skills—no matter how inexperienced a cook you are. Let's begin the tasting tour!

EASY COOKING DINNERS FOR 6

BUDGET ELEGANCE $20.00 or less

MENU:

Hors d'oeuvres

Brie, Jarlsberg, St. Marcellin, or other chèvre cheese
Crusty French bread and/or Canadian stoned wheat thins

Main Course

Black Bean Soup
Assorted breads with sweet butter

Condiments: sour cream with sliced scallions, chopped eggs, chopped onions, pepper-pickle relish, thin slices of lemon, cruet of light olive oil

Salad: Tomato-Cucumber Salad with Vinaigrette

Dessert

Lemon Sorbet with Sugar-Coated Zest of Fresh Lemons and Pepperidge Farm Pirouette cookies
Garnish top of sorbet with a Burton's leaf-shaped mint gumdrop

RECIPES:

Black Bean Soup
Tomato-Cucumber Salad with Vinaigrette
Sugar-Coated Zest of Fresh Lemons

[107]

Black Bean Soup (from scratch)

1½ pounds dried black beans
3 tablespoons olive oil
3 stalks celery, chopped fine
3 cloves garlic, minced
2 medium onions, chopped fine
parsley, 2 bay leaves, sprig of thyme
1 tomato, chopped
1 to 2 teaspoons oregano, crushed
5 to 6 shakes red-hot sauce
1 smoked ham hock
freshly ground salt and pepper, to taste
½ cup Madeira (or any sherrylike wine)

• Wash beans and soak overnight; remove imperfect ones.
• Heat olive oil in a 5- to 6-quart heavy pot and sauté celery, garlic, and onions.
• Add all ingredients except Madeira. Cook, covered, over low heat for 4 to 5 hours. (Prepare the day before and seasonings will blend better.)
• Remove bay leaves, parsley, and large pieces of thyme from beans, then pour into blender. Blend until consistency is even. Pass through a Foley mill, instead of blending, for more concentrated consistency.
• Add Madeira to purée and reheat.
• Serve with condiments.

Black Bean Soup (from a can)

• Heat 5 to 6 cans of soup over low heat.
• Add ½ cup Madeira, 3 tablespoons olive oil, 3 stalks celery, chopped fine.
• Garnish with sour cream and onions in individual servings.

Tomato-Cucumber Salad with Vinaigrette

5 medium tomatoes, thinly sliced
3 to 4 medium cucumbers, cut into long, thin sticks
½ cup Greek black olives

- Arrange tomato slices and cucumber sticks on individual plates.
- Garnish with olives.
- Dress with vinaigrette.

Vinaigrette (1 cup)

⅓ cup wine vinegar or fresh lemon juice
1 cup corn oil, olive oil, sesame oil, etc.
freshly ground salt and pepper, to taste
1 clove garlic, pressed (optional)

- Place all ingredients in 1-pint jar with lid and shake. Keeps well, so use as needed.

Variations: Consider adding shallots, basil, parsley, Dijon mustard, chives, or tarragon to the basic dressing recipe.

Sugar-Coated Zest of Fresh Lemons

2 fresh lemons
1 cup sugar

- Use lemon scorer or sharp knife to cut long julienne strips of yellow rind (no pith).
- Shake strips in covered jar of sugar until coated. Let dry on wax paper.

Putting Your Best Food Forward

*To transform this simple supper into a
beautiful feast, all you need is a dose of
cleverness and six loaves of bread!*

Buy six 8-inch round loaves of dark bread.

*Cut out a well in the center of each loaf,
large enough to hold a soup bowl. The bowl
should be even with the rim of the bread.*

*You may place the bread on a plate, a
wooden round, a cutting board, or directly on
the table top.*

*Garnish the soup with a dollop of sour
cream and a sprinkling of chopped parsley,
chives, or other condiments.*

*If you wish to carry out the look, serve
salad on ceramic plates and butter in
individual crockery pots.*

MODERATELY PRICED
$30.00 or less

MENU:

Hors d'oeuvres

Crab Meat Log with crackers

Main Course
Chicken New Orleans with Tomato Sauce Boats
Hot Buttered Rice
Boston or romaine lettuce with garlic vinaigrette

Dessert

Ice Cream Pie

RECIPES:

Crab Meat Log
Chicken New Orleans with Tomato Sauce Boats
Hot Buttered Rice
Ice Cream Pie

Crab Meat Log

8 ounces cream cheese, softened
6 scallions, thinly sliced
1 tablespoon Worcestershire sauce
1 cup chili sauce
1 tablespoon horseradish
3 to 4 shakes of Tabasco
1 package frozen crab or 1 can Harris Crab, drained
fresh lemon juice to taste
½ cup parsley, chopped

• Spread softened cream cheese, ⅛ to ¼ inch thick, onto a chilled serving plate that dips a little in the middle. (This keeps juices to the center.)
• Sprinkle scallions on layer of cheese, leaving about ½-inch border of cheese showing.
• Spread Worcestershire sauce, chili sauce, horseradish, and Tabasco over scallions.
• Cover with crab meat. Build up crab meat so it is in a large mound the length of the plate.
• Top with fresh lemon juice and parsley.
• Use butter spreader to scoop generous portions of all layers onto crackers.

Chicken New Orleans

1 tablespoon cooking oil
6 chicken breasts, skinned
⅓ cup green pepper, chopped
¼ cup celery, chopped
¾ cup onions, chopped coarsely
1 cup unpeeled carrots, thinly sliced
2 tablespoons tomato paste
¼ cup tomato sauce
½ cup port or white wine
2 cloves garlic, finely minced
pinch of thyme
12 ounces fresh mushrooms, sliced
3 tablespoons fresh parsley, minced
salt and pepper to taste

• Heat oil in heavy pot and brown chicken on both sides at medium heat.
• Add green peppers, celery, onions, and carrots; cover and cook about 10 minutes, stirring occasionally.
• Add tomato paste and sauce and cook another 5 minutes.
• Add remaining ingredients except parsley and cook, covered, 20 to 30 minutes.
• Add parsley last 10 minutes of cooking.
• Serve with or over hot buttered rice.

Tomato Sauce Boats

• Cut top fourth of tomato off. Tomato should be room temperature.
• Scoop out inside of tomatoes. Leave sides and walls solid.
• Fill each tomato with sauce from the chicken.
• Replace tops on tomatoes.
• Serve one tomato on each dinner place. Uncap just before eating.

Hot Buttered Rice

1¼ cups rice
2¼ cups water
3 tablespoons butter
2 teaspoons salt

• Bring butter-salted water to boil in heavy pot and add rice.
• Bring to rolling boil once more.
• Cover pot and reduce to low heat and cook 20 minutes, or until tender and fluffy.
• To keep rice moist and warm until ready to serve, butter a piece of brown paper the diameter of pot and place over rice. Then cover with lid; holds very nicely.

Ice Cream Pie

1 cup evaporated milk
6 ounces semi-sweet chocolate chips
1 cup miniature marshmallows
vanilla wafers
1½ quarts vanilla ice cream (allow ice cream to soften at room temperature)
½ cup toasted pecans

• Make chocolate sauce by combining evaporated milk and chocolate chips in saucepan and heating until melted. Add marshmallows and stir until dissolved.

• Line 9- or 10-inch glass pie pan—bottom and sides—with one layer of vanilla wafers.
• Spread half the softened ice cream over top; then spread layer of half the chocolate sauce.
• Repeat; sprinkle toasted pecan halves over top.
• Cover tightly and freeze. Place in refrigerator just before dinner. It'll be perfect texture when ready for dessert!

Variation: If you don't have a pie plate, put a scoop of ice cream on a bed of wafers on individual serving plates. Top with sauce and pecans.

PUTTING YOUR BEST FOOD FORWARD

To make Chicken New Orleans as festive as Mardi Gras, just try these simple techniques.

Serve the chicken on individual plates. Arrange them in the kitchen and bring to table.

Place half a chicken breast on each plate. Coat with a very small amount of sauce.

Cut tops off six ripe, red tomatoes. Scoop out inside pulp. Spoon sauce from chicken into each tomato. Recap.

Put one tomato sauce boat on each plate.
Garnish plate with a leaf of soft, green
Boston lettuce placed under the tomato or the
chicken, or with a sprig of watercress or
parsley around the outside of the tomato.
Rice may be served from a bowl on the
table or put on each plate in the kitchen.
Remember to balance the plate,
arranging food with regard
to shape, color, and texture.

To present the dessert
at the table or around
a coffee table in the
living room, take the time
to try these simple garnishes.
If possible, use an elevated cake stand.
Search garage sales and flea markets for old
glass or white china ones. If you do not have
a cake stand, garnish a flat platter as
described below.

Arrange a fringe of shiny, deep green lemon
leaves around the edge of the plate. Secure
them to the plate with Scotch tape. Place a
round white paper doily in the center of the
plate so that it covers the taped ends of the
leaves. It should not extend beyond the edge of
the pie.

WOWZIE DINNER
$35.00 or more

MENU:

Hors d'oeuvres

Baked Camembert with crusty French bread and sweet butter

Main Course

Garlic Pork or Beef Roast
Pan-Roasted Potatoes
Creamed Spinach

Escarole and water chestnuts with sesame vinaigrette

Dessert

Crême Chantilly with Raspberry Sauce

RECIPES:

Baked Camembert
Garlic Roast
Pan-Roasted Potatoes
Creamed Spinach
Crême Chantilly with Raspberry Sauce

Baked Camembert

two 4-inch rounds or one 10-inch round ripe Camembert
1 to 2 teaspoons caraway seeds, optional

- Chill cheese thoroughly.
- Slice off the top crust of cheese with a sharp, thin knife, leaving the remaining crust as a bowl.
- Sprinkle caraway seeds over top of cheese and place on a platter from which you plan to serve.

• Bake at no higher than 350° until melted through; about 20 minutes for 4-inch rounds.
• Scoop cheese with teaspoon or spreader onto French bread or fresh apple slices.

Tip: Hot cheese returns to solid state once cooled, so place on a buffet warming unit if available.

Garlic Roast

One 4- to 5-pound pork loin roast or beef rib roast
2 garlic cloves, slivered
medium-coarse black pepper and salt
3 tablespoons cornstarch
1 cup cold water
(use 1 teaspoon meat tenderizer for lower-grade meats)

• Have butcher crack along ribs for easy carving.
• Make small incisions in roast and insert garlic slivers at random.
• Season generously with salt and pepper.
• Combine cornstarch and water (and tenderizer). Pour over roast and let sit at room temperature for 1 to 2 hours.
• Drain off marinade and cook roast uncovered.
• If cooking pork: preheat oven to 325°. Cook meat 35 to 45 minutes per pound.
• If cooking beef: preheat oven to 450°. Cook at that temperature for 20 minutes, then turn down oven to 325° and cook until roast is done. (Allow 15 to 18 minutes per pound for rare, 18 to 20 minutes for medium.) Let roast stand at room temperature for 15 minutes before carving.

Pan-Roasted Potatoes

2 pounds small, new red potatoes—at least 2 per person
¼ cup butter
1 teaspoon cooking oil
salt and pepper, to taste
1 teaspoon seasoned salt, optional

• Cook potatoes in boiling, salted water for 10 minutes. Drain and skin.
• Heat butter and oil in a pan 13 by 9 by 2 inches. Add skinned potatoes, turning to coat with butter.
• Season and bake uncovered at 325°, turning once, for 35 to 40 minutes.

Creamed Spinach

3 pounds fresh spinach, or 3 packages frozen chopped spinach
1 stick unsalted butter
½ cup heavy cream
salt, white pepper, to taste
pinch of freshly ground nutmeg

• Wash spinach several times in sink to remove sand and insects. (A drop of vinegar in water takes care of insects). Dry spinach; remove stems.
• Chop *coarsely*.
• If using frozen spinach, thaw packages and drop into salted, boiling water and cook at rolling boil for 2 to 3 minutes, uncovered. Strain; rinse in cold water and drain completely. (Squeeze with palms of hands.)
• Melt butter in large skillet until bubbly.
• Toss spinach in butter until all butter is absorbed.
• Season and add cream; heat through.
• Adjust seasoning.
• Top with freshly ground nutmeg and serve.

Crême Chantilly with Raspberry Sauce

2 cups or 1 pint heavy cream
2 tablespoons superfine or powdered sugar
1 tablespoon kirsch, cognac, or vanilla
1 quart fresh raspberries or 2 packages frozen, well drained

• Chill bowl and beaters.
• Beat cream until it starts to thicken. Add sugar and flavoring and beat until it forms soft peaks.

• Place in paper-towel-lined strainer over a bowl and chill. Cream will hold for about 2 hours; this allows excess liquid to drain off cream.
• To serve, fold berries into cream and place in goblets.
• Top with toasted macaroon crumbs or serve with whole cookies.

PUTTING YOUR BEST FOOD FORWARD

To transform a roast from a heavy, dull slab of meat into a fanciful, appealing main dish, garnish the plate as shown in the illustration.
Use small lemon leaves (or endive) to create a textured fringe all around the platter.
Surround the meat with small cherry tomatoes, whole white mushrooms, even water chestnuts. You can interlace strips of scallions or red or green pepper if you wish. Keep in mind the blend of flavors and the excitement that color contrast creates.
When carving and serving the meat, arrange slices on plate in a way that re-creates the look of the serving platter. Place two leaves on the edge of the platter and top with one tomato and each of the other garnishes.

I WON'T COOK DINNER FOR 6

TAKEOUT DINNER DELIGHTS

MENU:

Spareribs, Sweet and Sour Shrimp, Chicken with Cashews (or Moo Goo Gai Pan), Moo Shu Pork (or a beef dish), Buddhist Delight Vegetables, Rice or Noodles

Ice Cream and Ginger Cookies
(Fortune cookies are fun! If time permits, the hostess can write up fortunes with her special guests in mind.)

PUTTING THEIR BEST FOOD FORWARD

When you use takeout food for a dinner party, you should apply the same care with its presentation as you would if you had made it yourself. If you've chosen a Chinese takeout meal, consider creating an Oriental-style table.

Use a large, folding parasol as a table arrangement. Place it at one end of the table and spread the food dishes out from under it—like an upside-down cornucopia.

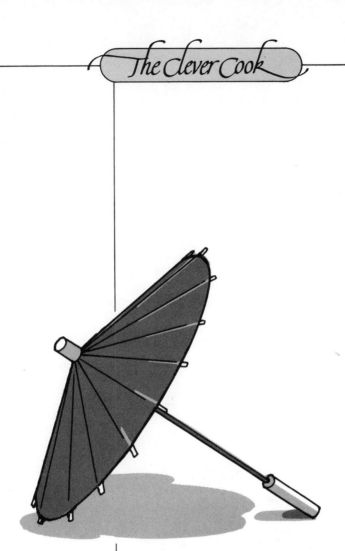

Dress up each serving bowl with a large tea or banana leaf. Make sure it drapes over the edge of the bowl. Mound up the food so it does not look sloppy. You may want to garnish the top of each dish with some fresh Chinese vegetables. Create a sunburst from snow pea pods or decorate spareribs with thin orange slices that create a scalloped edge along the rim of the bowl. By adding a fresh touch, the takeout food looks as if it came from **your** kitchen—not theirs!

[121]

COCKTAILS AND HORS D'OEUVRES FOR 20

BUDGET ELEGANCE
Food: $20.00 or less
Beverage: $20.00 or more

MENU:

Two Cold Pastas:

Rigatoni with Fresh Tomato Sauce
Shells with Spinach "Pesto" Sauce

(Using Cabbage Head)
Raw vegetables with mustard-mayonnaise and Roquefort Dip

Hot Cheese Canapés
Assorted breads and sweet butter

Beverage:

Bloody Marys

RECIPES:

Pasta
Roquefort Dip
Fresh Tomato Sauce
Spinach "Pesto" Sauce
Hot Cheese Canapés

Pasta

1 pound pasta, shells, rigatoni, rotini, etc.
1 to 2 tablespoons olive oil
2 tablespoons salt
6 quarts water

- Bring water, oil, and salt to rolling boil. Add pasta and cook until al dente, or just tender, about 10 minutes.
- Remove from heat immediately and rinse with cold water. Drain. Toss with 1 tablespoon olive oil.
- Toss warm pasta with cold sauce.

Roquefort Dip

3 to 4 ounces Roquefort cheese, crumbled
1½ cups mayonnaise
¼ cup vinegar
salt, white pepper, and cayenne, to taste
sugar to taste

• Combine all ingredients and let season several hours.

Fresh Tomato Sauce

6 medium tomatoes
3 cloves garlic, pressed
2 teaspoons basil, crushed
1 pinch sugar
2 tablespoons lemon juice
¾ cup olive oil
freshly ground salt and pepper, to taste

• Peel, seed, and chop tomatoes, retaining juices.
• Combine with other ingredients and let season at least two hours.
• Mix with hot pasta, garnish with minced parsley, and serve.

(A great way to use any leftover is to cover with fresh Parmesan and bake for Sunday supper; a little yoghurt or sour cream with chives makes this dish a delightful summer salad!)

Spinach "Pesto" Sauce

4 to 5 cloves garlic, finely minced
5 cups or 1½ pounds fresh spinach and a little coarse salt
1¼ cups fresh Parmesan or Romano cheese
2 to 3 tablespoons olive oil, enough to give desired consistency
freshly ground pepper, to taste
¼ cup toasted pine nuts or cherry tomatoes for garnish

• Blend or process garlic; add spinach gradually, until a rough paste is formed. It should not be completely smooth.
• Incorporate Parmesan or Romano.
• Dilute with olive oil. Correct seasoning.
• Toss hot pasta in bowl and coat with sauce. Garnish with pine nuts or cherry tomatoes.

(This makes a lovely hot casserole by adding heavy cream to the "Pesto" mixture and topping with fresh Parmesan; heat until cheese melts.)

Hot Cheese Canapés

1 loaf sandwich bread
two 3-ounce packages cream cheese
2 egg yolks, beaten
1 tablespoon onion, finely minced
mayonnaise, enough to get spreading consistency
Worcestershire sauce, cayenne pepper, and salt, to taste

• Remove crusts from bread. Cut into 1-inch strips, 4 squares, doughnut holes, or any shape you desire. Toast one side of bread in broiler.
• Combine remaining ingredients and spread generously onto untoasted side of the bread shapes.
• Broil until bubbly and golden.

(These can be made in advance and frozen. To serve, let thaw 1 hour and bake at 350° for 5 minutes.)

COCKTAIL BUFFET FOR 20

MODERATELY PRICED
Food: $30.00 or less
Beverage: $30.00 or more

MENU:

Marinated Vegetables
Salmon Pâté
Chinese Chicken
Chutney Cheese Ball
Assorted breads and crackers
Assorted butter cookies or
    dark and light chocolates (or both)

Beverage:

White wine spritzers

RECIPES:

Marinated Vegetables
Salmon Pâté
Chinese Chicken
Chutney Cheese Ball

Marinated Vegetables

1 can green olives
1 can black olives
1 head fresh cauliflower
1 pound small fresh mushrooms; leave whole
1 pint cherry tomatoes
½ pound carrots, peeled and cut into strips
½ bunch celery, cut into strips
1½ cups vegetable oil
⅔ cup white vinegar
salt, to taste
1 teaspoon freshly ground pepper
2 to 3 minced garlic cloves

- Drain olives and prepare vegetables in bite-size pieces.
- Combine oil, vinegar, and seasonings in a blender.
- Pour over vegetables and marinate overnight.

PUTTING YOUR BEST FOOD FORWARD

For housewarming parties, or if you just lack a buffet, consider this unique party look.

Take a sturdy stepladder. You may want to decorate its legs with strands of ivy, but, as you can see in the drawing, this isn't necessary.

Create a bountiful vegetable tray to put on the paint holder on the back of the ladder.

Buy one large head of cabbage—white or red—with all the outside leaves still attached.

Wash well. Cut a deep well into the center of the head.

Put your dip bowl into this well.

Spread out the outer leaves and peel back a few of the inner ones to create a ruffled collar around the cabbage.

Slice a variety of vegetables—carrots, broccoli, zucchini, scallions, cauliflower, peppers—in strips, rounds, wedges, florets.

Arrange these vegetables on the cabbage leaves and the platter surrounding the cabbage. Keep in mind the textures, shapes, and colors of the vegetables, and vary the height and shape of the overall arrangement.

Put the cold pasta in a square lacquered tray on the top step of the ladder. Keep pastas separated so flavors do not blur. Place leafy barriers of lettuce around each one.

Fill in the remaining steps with breads and butters. You may want to put napkins, plates, and flatware on the ladder or nearby.

Salmon Pâté

1 envelope unflavored gelatin
¼ cup water
1 can red salmon, drained and skin removed
½ cup celery, finely minced
¼ cup green pepper
3 tablespoons onions, finely minced
1 hard-cooked egg, finely minced
salt, white pepper, cayenne, to taste
⅓ cup mayonnaise
sour cream and mayonnaise for topping

- Dissolve gelatin in water and then place over a pan of water and heat until gelatin is completely dissolved.
- Combine remaining ingredients, folding in the mayonnaise.
- Pour into a greased 8-inch ring mold and chill.
- Top with mixture of sour cream and mayonnaise.

Chinese Chicken

2 cloves garlic, minced
20 to 25 chicken wings cut in half at joint; wing tips removed and saved for making stock
fresh ginger root, about 1-inch piece, minced
½ cup soy sauce
½ cup vermouth
cayenne pepper, to taste
2 to 3 tablespoons peanut oil
⅓ cup Hoisin sauce and enough additional soy sauce to make a "paint" or glaze for chicken

- Combine all ingredients except Hoisin sauce and let marinate a couple of hours or overnight.
- Place in an aluminum-foil-lined pan and bake at 400° for 30 to 40 minutes, turning only once.
- Brush chicken with heated Hoisin-soy sauce glaze when removing from oven. Serve hot.

Note: You may use drumsticks, thighs, or chunks of chicken breasts.

Chutney Cheese Ball (makes 2 balls)

16 ounces cream cheese
10 ounces sharp cheddar cheese, grated
1 to 2 tablespoons curry powder
Worcestershire sauce
garlic salt
Tabasco sauce
salt and white pepper
3 to 4 green onions, thinly sliced
½ cup chutney

- Combine the 2 cheeses until blended.
- Add curry powder and other spices according to taste.
- Form into 2 patties (like a hamburger).
- Sprinkle onions over cheese.
- Top with chutney.
- Serve with bite-size crackers.

PUTTING YOUR BEST FOOD FORWARD

For an outdoor cocktail buffet or a casual indoor gathering, try these presentation tricks.

Serve the chicken in a double hibachi. Use thin metal skewers to hold chicken in place. Arrange wings in alternating patterns. If you wish, you may place a few glowing briquettes in the hibachi to keep chicken warm while serving. Place foil pierced with a few holes over briquettes to keep chicken from burning.

Arrange marinated vegetables on a full head of cauliflower. If possible, get one with its outer leaves still attached. If not, use red leaf or bib lettuce around the cauliflower to re-create that look.

Stud the head with vegetables on toothpicks. Keep a supply of vegetables on toothpicks in the refrigerator so you can replenish the arrangement as it is eaten.

WOWZIE BUFFET
Food: $60.00 or less
Beverage: $40.00 or more

MENU:

Chicken teriyaki chunks on skewers
Lobster Newburg with chunks of French bread
Ratatouille in miniature pita bread pockets
Beef Tenderloin on rye

Beverage:

Champagne. Try an inexpensive Blanc de Blanc or the Spanish bubbly Friexenet in clear or black bottle.

RECIPES:

Lobster Newburg
Ratatouille
Beef Tenderloin
Rich Chocolate Cake

Lobster Newburg

2 packages frozen Stouffers Welsh Rarebit
1 package Stouffers Lobster Newburg
1 teaspoon cayenne pepper and white pepper
Salt, to taste
⅓ cup sherry
¾ pound fresh lobster or shrimp

- Place all frozen foods in heavy pot and let thaw.
- Add seasonings and heat until blended and of dipping consistency. (Add milk if too thick.)
- Add fresh lobster or shrimp just before serving and heat through.
- Serve from chafing dish.

Ratatouille

5 medium size zucchini
1 medium eggplant
2 green peppers
2 medium onions
2 cloves garlic, finely minced
6 tablespoons olive oil
Freshly ground salt and pepper, thyme, and pinch of sugar,
  to taste
1 29-ounce can of tomatoes or 2 pounds fresh tomatoes,
  peeled and chopped

- Peel eggplant and cut into 1-inch squares.
- Cut zucchini into 1-inch squares also.
- Place eggplant and zucchini in a colander and sprinkle with salt (to withdraw excess water before cooking). Let sit 20 to 30 minutes.
- Chop onions coarsely; cut green peppers into 1-inch squares and set aside.
- Heat olive oil in a large heavy pot; sauté onions and garlic until soft—don't brown. Remove.
- Add zucchini and eggplant to oil and cook about 5 minutes, tossing and coating vegetables with oil.
- Return garlic and onions and other ingredients to pot and cook uncovered over low heat until vegetables are al dente or a nice melange. This can be served hot or cold, and it can be made the day before so that flavors blend. (Ratatouille is also nice over linguine or in a hot baked potato.)

Beef Tenderloin (serves 20 for cocktails)

2 beef tenderloins, about 3 to 4 pounds each, larded
freshly ground pepper, to taste
1 bottle La Choy brown gravy sauce
fresh parsley, for garnish

- Have tenderloin at room temperature and season with pepper.
- Pour ½ bottle brown gravy sauce over larding on each tenderloin.

• Roast in 400° oven for 45 minutes for rare. (If tenderloins are small, reduce heat to 350° for last 15 minutes.)
• Remove from oven and let rest 15 minutes.
• Slice thinly, garnish with fresh parsley, and serve on thin rye, coated with Dijon mustard. Or make a spread of 1 pint whipped cream and 3 or 4 table-spoons horseradish.

(This can be served hot or cold.)

Rich Chocolate Cake

Batter
2 cups flour
2 cups sugar
1 stick butter
½ cup cooking oil
1 cup water
4 tablespoons cocoa
1 teaspoon soda
½ cup buttermilk
2 beaten eggs
1 teaspoon vanilla

• Combine sugar and flour in a large bowl.
• Combine next 4 ingredients in saucepan and bring to a boil. Stir constantly.
• Combine dry ingredients with boiled mixture and mix well.
• Dissolve soda in buttermilk; add eggs and vanilla to above mixture and mix well.
• Pour into 9- by 13-inch greased cake pan and bake 30 to 35 minutes at 350°. (Can also be baked in a 15 x 10½ x 1-inch pan.)
• Make frosting.

Frosting
3 tablespoons cocoa
6 tablespoons canned milk
1 stick butter
1 box confectioners sugar, sifted
1 teaspoon vanilla

PUTTING YOUR BEST FOOD FORWARD

For a wowzie presentation of your wowzie cocktail buffet, you can haul out the old silver service that's been hiding in the cupboard. No silver? No problem. Use a large casserole or platter to create this look.

Arrange chicken teriyaki chunks on thin wooden skewers.

Alternate chicken with pieces of pineapple, peppers, mango, or tomatoes.

Create a fresh-fruit frieze along the back of the serving dish. Cut a pineapple in half, lengthwise. Use it as the centerpiece of the arrangement. Place fresh fruit all around it. Use grapes, berries, anything in season.

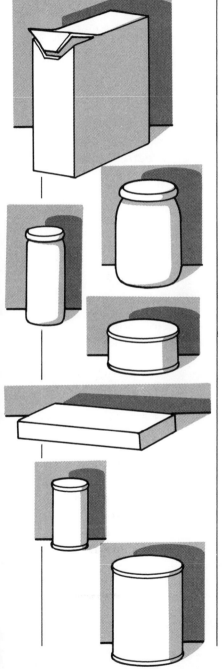

- Bring first 3 ingredients to a boil; stir constantly.
- Remove from heat.
- Add sugar; beat well.
- Pour over cake while still warm.

Variation:
Sprinkle 1 cup coarsely chopped pecans over the
   warm frosting.

OFF THE SHELF

Non-cooks, busy cooks, gourmets, and last minute
entertainers can all have an easier time of it if they learn
to put together intriguing dishes by relying on creative
shortcuts.

There are a thousand and one ways to stock your
shelves so that you don't have to make a big deal out of
every course of your party menu. If you are confident
that you can put a special taste treat together easily and
quickly with what you have on hand, you never need to
panic when you burn the appetizers (or the entrée!), an
extra guest shows up, or your lover brings home the
boss—without any notice.

CUPBOARD
CACHES

Soups such as: bouillon, chicken and beef broth,
tomato soup, mushroom soup, and clam broth.

Canned fish and meat such as: tinned pâté, smoked
oysters, clams, white meat tuna in water, salmon,
sardines, herring in glass jars, or anchovies.

Vegetables such as: artichoke hearts, beets in glass
jars, baby peas, bamboo, water chestnuts, tomatoes
(whole, puréed, pâté, sauces), mushrooms, and
olives—ripe and green.

Pasta: any or all varieties of noodles, spaghetti,
macaroni.

Juices.

Canned fruits such as: apricot, peaches, and Mandarin oranges.

Sauces: dried Italian salad dressing mix, mustards (mild, hot), special flavors, gravies, and barbeque sauce.

There are a thousand and one ways to use these handy Off the Shelf items. Following are some sample suggestions for creating instant first courses, entrées, and desserts.

CANNED MEAT AND FISH

Dried Beef

Consider using this for:
Cocktail spreads, canapés, or dips
Stuffing for eggs, meats, or vegetables
Sandwiches—hot, cold, or open-faced
Main course for breakfast, brunch, or light supper

Crab Meat

Consider using crab for:
Cocktail spreads, hors d'oeuvres, and dips
Salads or pasta sauces

Hot Chipped Beef Dip (serves 8)

½ cup pecans, coarsely chopped
2 tablespoons butter
½ teaspoon salt
one 8-ounce package cream cheese, softened
2 tablespoons milk
one 2½ ounce jar dried beef, torn in small pieces
¼ cup green pepper, finely chopped
2 tablespoons grated onion, or dried
½ teaspoon garlic salt
white and cayenne pepper, to taste
½ cup sour cream

• Toast pecans with salt and butter in 325° oven. Remove and cool.
• Combine remaining ingredients, except sour cream; fold in the sour cream and half the nuts.
• Pour into a greased 8-inch porcelain quiche pan or two 4-inch ramekins; bake for 20 minutes at 350°.
• Serve hot with crackers.

VEGETABLES

Artichokes

Consider using for:
Hot and cold hors d'oeuvres, spreads, and pâtés
Salads with fruits, other vegetables, meats, and cheese
Vegetable dish—creamed, boiled, sautéed, puréed, or in vegetable casserole
Main course with eggs, shrimp, crab meat
Stuffing for meats and vegetables

Chick Peas

Consider using for:
Dip for vegetables or crusty bread
Salad or vegetable alone or with other vegetables
Stews, soups, casseroles of Spanish, Moroccan, Middle Eastern or Indian flavor

RECIPES:

Party Shrimp and Artichokes
Spanish Chick Pea Soup

Party Shrimp and Artichokes (serves 5)

7 tablespoons butter
8 ounces fresh mushrooms, sliced
4 tablespoons flour
¾ cup milk
¾ cup heavy cream
one 14-ounce can artichokes, drained
1 pound shrimp, barely cooked
1 tablespoon Worcestershire
¼ cup dry sherry
¼ cup fresh Parmesan, grated

• Melt 3 tablespoons butter in saucepan and sauté mushrooms for about 5 minutes. Set aside.
• Melt remaining 4 tablespoons butter in pan, add flour, and cook 2 to 3 minutes, stirring constantly.
• Add milk and cream and cook over low heat until thick and smooth (don't boil!).
• Place artichokes in bottom of a greased 1½-quart casserole; layer with shrimp and then mushrooms.
• Add Worcestershire and sherry to sauce and pour over dish.
• Sprinkle with Parmesan and bake at 375° for 20 to 25 minutes.
• Serve with or over hot rice and a salad.

Spanish Chick Pea Soup (serves 8)

2 tablespoons olive oil
1 clove garlic, minced
1 cup onions, coarsely chopped
½ cup boiled or cooked ham, diced
½ pound chorizos or Polish sausage, diced
2 cans chick peas, rinsed and drained
two 13-ounce cans chicken broth
1 bay leaf
two 8-ounce cans tomato sauce
4 cups water
1 cup carrots, pared and sliced
freshly ground salt and pepper, to taste

- Heat olive oil in a 6-quart pan and sauté garlic and onions until tender but not browned.
- Add ham and chorizos or sausage and cook about 5 minutes.
- Add remaining ingredients and cook, covered, until carrots and chick peas are tender.
- Serve with tossed salad and hard rolls for an easy, hearty lunch or supper.

SOUPS

Tomato Soup

Consider using for:
Appetizers and spreads
Base for heartier soups, stews, casseroles, and meat loafs
Molded salads or salad dressings
Meat glazes and sauces
Vegetable marinade or sauce

Chicken Broth

Consider using for:
Appetizers, hot or cold
Base for heartier soups, stews, and casseroles
Enriching potatoes, rice, sauces, or gravies
Congealing with vegetables or meats

RECIPES:

Hot Curry Soup
Greek Lemon Soup

Hot Curry Soup (serves 8)

1 can beef bouillon
1 can plain pea soup
1 can tomato soup
1 can water
1 teaspoon fresh curry powder, or more
3 wedges of lemon, to be cooked
thin slices of lemon, for garnish

• Combine all ingredients, except slices of lemon for garnish, until smooth and hot.
• Serve in heavy mugs with lemon slice on top.

Greek Lemon Soup (Avgolemono Soup) (serves 6 to 8)

3 cans chicken broth or 6 cups chicken stock
¼ cup long grain rice
1 teaspoon salt
3 eggs
¼ cup fresh lemon juice
1 slice lemon per serving, as garnish

• Combine broth, rice, and salt in large saucepan and bring to boil. Reduce heat; cover and simmer until rice is just tender, about 15 minutes.
• Remove pan from heat.
• Beat eggs in a bowl until fluffy and pale yellow. Beat in the lemon juice.
• Slowly stir 2 cups hot broth into the egg-lemon mixture and whisk vigorously as you pour.
• Pour the egg mixture slowly back into the broth-rice mixture, whisking mixture as you pour.
• Serve cold with lemon slices or fresh mint, or serve hot. (If serving hot, heat at low temperature so the eggs don't curdle.)

CANNED FRUIT

Mandarin Oranges

Consider using as:
Appetizer as fruit cup or hors d'oeuvres
Salad with other fruits, spinach, avocados, and onions
Glazes for chicken, pork, squash, or sweet potatoes
Dessert topping for ice cream, cakes, or puddings

Pineapple Chunks

Consider using for:
Appetizers and hors d'oeuvres, hot or cold
Side dishes and garnishes for pork, ham, or chicken
Fruit salads, congealed or compote type
Hot or cold dessert with other fruits, cakes, ice cream,
or boiled custards

RECIPES:

Mandarin Orange Sauce
for Ice Cream or Chicken
Escalloped Pineapple

Mandarin Orange Sauce for Ice Cream or Chicken (makes 1½ cups)

1 can mandarin oranges, drained, and juice reserved
fresh orange juice to make 1½ cups
2 teaspoons arrowroot
2 tablespoons sugar
2 teaspoons curry powder
2 teaspoons fresh orange zest
1 to 2 tablespoons lemon juice, to taste
½ cup raisins
½ cup white wine
½ cup walnuts, optional
dash of orange food coloring, optional

• Marinate or "plump" raisins in white wine. Set aside.
• Combine juices with arrowroot. Then cook over medium heat until mixture starts to thicken; stir constantly.
• Add remaining ingredients and cook 3 to 5 minutes.

Variations:
• For ice cream, substitute cinnamon for curry powder.
• For chicken, salt and pepper chicken generously. Place chicken in an aluminum-foil-lined casserole. Pour sauce and nuts over top. Cover with foil. Bake at 400° for 15 minutes. Reduce heat to 350° and bake 30 minutes. Remove foil from top, baste with sauce, and bake final 15 minutes. Great with rice and a salad.

Escalloped Pineapple (serves 6 to 8)

1½ cups sugar
½ pound butter
2 eggs
½ cup milk
5 slices bread, crusts removed and cubed
2¼ cups or two 15-ounce cans pineapple cubes plus the juices

• Cream sugar and butter; add remaining ingredients and toss together.
• Pour into an oblong pan 9 by 13 inches and bake for 1 hour at 350°.

(This can be served as a dessert or as a side dish with ham, pork, or chicken.)

JUICES

Orange Juice

Consider using for:
Appetizers—chilled, mixed with other juices, wines, vodka, champagne, rum
Marinade for fresh fruits, meats, and poultry
Sauces and glazes for fruits—apples and oranges; vegetables—sweet potatoes, acorn squash; meats—chicken, duck, and pork
Dessert such as frozen ice, a sauce or glaze for cakes, puddings, and fillings.

Tomato Juice

Consider using for:
Appetizer—hot, cold, spicy; with other juices or liquors
Congealed salads and marinade for vegetables
Liquid and seasoning for gumbos, stews, casseroles, and vegetable dishes

RECIPES:

Orange Ice
Molded Gazpacho

Orange Ice (serves 4)

zest (peel) from one fresh orange
4 cups orange juice
1 cup sugar
⅓ cup Grand Marnier
fresh mint or cherry, as garnish

- Remove yellow zest from fresh orange, either with a zester or a sharp knife.
- Blend or process zest until finely minced.
- Add 1 cup of juice, the sugar, and Grand Marnier.
- Blend or process until combined.
- Blend in remaining juice. Pour into 2 ice cube freezer trays and freeze.
- Just before serving, blend or process orange cubes until a fine ice. Serve immediately in sherbet or cocktail glasses. Very light and refreshing.

Molded Gazpacho (serves 6 to 8)

5 packages unflavored gelatin
one 46-ounce can tomato juice
2 large tomatoes, peeled and seeded
1 small onion, quartered
1 medium cucumber, peeled and seeded
2 to 3 fresh scallions, finely chopped
2 tablespoons lemon juice
6 tablespoons olive oil
2 tablespoons wine vinegar
1 teaspoon salt and celery salt
white pepper, Tabasco, and Worcestershire sauce, to taste
sour cream, for topping

- In a large saucepan, soften gelatin with ½ can of tomato juice. Simmer until dissolved. Let cool a little.
- Blend or process tomatoes, small onion, and cucumber until puréed.
- Add blended vegetables and remaining ingredients to lukewarm gelatin mixture.
- Pour into greased 1½-quart mold and chill.
- Unmold; fill center with crab, shrimp, or cottage cheese; or top each serving with a little sour cream.

The Clever Cook

SAUCES AND FLAVORINGS

Worcestershire Sauce

Consider using as flavoring in:
Appetizer foods and drinks, both hot and cold
Seafood, meats, vegetables, gumbos, and stews
Sauces for hot or chilled seafood, beef, pork, or poultry

Chutney

Consider using as a condiment with:
Eggs, cheese, and nuts; lamb, chicken, pork, beef, or potatoes
Hot or cold sandwiches

RECIPES:

Barbecued Pork Chops
Chutney Cheese Spread

Barbecued Pork Chops (serves 2 to 4)

(Easy company dish to prepare and forget!)

4 pork loin chops, ¾ to 1 inch thick
2 tablespoons oil
1 medium onion, thinly sliced
¾ cup catsup
1 tablespoon vinegar
¾ cup water
1 tablespoon Worcestershire sauce, or more
1 teaspoon fresh chili powder
1 teaspoon fresh paprika
¼ to ½ teaspoon cayenne pepper

- Brown chops in hot oil and place in a casserole.
- Place sliced onion over chops; combine remaining ingredients and pour over chops and onions.

- Bake uncovered at 400° for about 1 hour.

Note: This is enough sauce for 4 chops only. If preparing more, double the recipe.)

Chutney Cheese Spread

2 cups cheddar cheese, shredded
½ cup Major Grey's Chutney, finely minced
1 to 2 scallions, thinly sliced

- Combine all ingredients and use:
to top a nice, hot, fluffy baked potato
to stuff a pita bread pocket filled with slices of cold lamb, chicken, or pork
to spread over broiled chicken the last 5 minutes of broiling—skin side up.

HERBS AND SPICES

Cumin

This special spice jazzes up:
Appetizers with cheese, eggs, or chicken
Main courses of kibbee, lamb, chicken, or chili
Vegetables such as okra, green beans, potatoes, or sauerkraut
Dessert cakes and breads

Ginger

Consider using ginger in:
Appetizers or main courses as marinade flavoring or in sauces for chicken, beef, pork, chicken livers, fish, water chestnuts, or fruits
Carrots, sweet potatoes, or squash
Desserts such as pies, puddings, cakes, custards, sauces, or ice cream

RECIPES:

Middle Eastern Green Beans
Ginger Ice Cream with Peaches

Middle Eastern Green Beans (serves 4 to 6)

1 to 2 tablespoons olive oil
2 cloves garlic, finely minced
2 medium onions, coarsely chopped
½ pound ground lamb
1 teaspoon freshly ground salt, pepper, and cumin powder, or more
one 28-ounce can tomatoes, broken up
one 37-ounce can cut green beans, rinsed in cold water and drained

- Sauté garlic and onion in large pot.
- Add ground lamb; brown and drain excess grease.
- Put remaining ingredients into pot and cook until seasonings are blended, about 30 minutes.
- Serve in soup bowl over hot rice with French bread and butter.

Ginger Ice Cream with Peaches (serves 4 to 6)

1 quart vanilla ice cream
1 teaspoon powdered ginger, or more

- Let ice cream soften a little; blend ginger throughout and refreeze.
- Serve with additional ginger sprinkled on top; with sugar cookies; topped with partially thawed frozen peaches.

"Compassion soothes the savage guest."

CHAPTER •11•

LIQUID ASSETS

No matter what type of party you are throwing, you need to provide ample liquid refreshment for your guests. But you do not have to rival the corner bar. You do not have to offer your guests every imaginable beverage.

These days, more and more people are drinking light. White wine spritzers and light beers are favorites. And it's about time. As with food, the operating rule for drinks is quality and style, not quantity.

This is good news because it means you can spare your budget without being stingy. A "one-liquor bar" is both stylish and economical. Wine, punch, or a batch of Bloody Marys is sufficient. Stick with basics; keep service simple. The keys to a successful bar are the menu and the service. Let's look at these two components and see how you can make the most of your liquid assets.

GENERAL RULES FOR BAR SERVICE

• Make sure every arriving guest has a drink (and something to nibble) as soon as he or she enters the party. People are more at ease when they can busy their hands. The initial awkwardness of entering a room is diminished. And, face it, a little liquor calms the nerves and loosens the tongue.

• The bar setup should always be separated from the food service. For large parties, place them in different rooms, if possible.

• If serving drinks before dinner, close the bar when you call your guests to the table. After dinner, drinks can be served at the table or from a coffee table in the living room. It is not necessary to have an open bar all evening.

• If serving wine as a cocktail, make sure it

goes with the meal as well. Have guests bring glasses to the table when it is time to eat.

• The drinks should complement the mood of the evening and the flavor of the food.

• When offering your guests a drink, guide their choice by telling them what's available. Don't put yourself, or your guest, in the embarrassing position of not having what's requested.

• During larger gatherings, don't take yourself out of the party by standing behind the bar. You can set up a self-service bar or have it manned by a friend, a mate, or a hired helper. For six or fewer guests, you can leave the room temporarily to mix their drinks.

• Offer a wide selection of nonalcoholic beverages at any gathering.

• Never force a drink on a guest.

SETTING UP A BAR

As we discovered in Chap-

ter 6, "New Uses for Old Spaces," you can set up a bar in the bedroom, or bathroom, on a desk or a coffee table. Where you choose to set it up depends on the size of your home and how large a bar you need. For small dinners, a living room, coffee table, or card table will do; for a medium-sized buffet, you might use a dresser top; for a big cocktail party or late-night fete, you might set up two bars at opposite ends of the house. But whatever you do, there are some basic techniques you can use so that you've got plenty of ice and good spirits.

Supplies

Keep on hand in your kitchen for use on bar if needed:

• Two corkscrews
• Bottle opener
• Jigger measurer
• Three large carafes to decant wine or liquor, or to use for ice water
• Small white cocktail napkins
• Four or more large glass ashtrays. Never use small ones!

• Coasters, coasters, and more coasters. Put them around on any surface you want to protect.
• Paring knife
• Ice pick
• Wine coolers
• Ice buckets of various sizes

Condiments for Bar

Lemons (slices and twists)
Limes
Onions
Olives
Cherries
Oranges
Pineapple sticks
Cucumber sticks
Celery
Bitters
Tonic and soda

Glassware

Plan on two or three glasses per guest. The larger the party, the more glasses you'll need. Don't feel you must have five different styles of barware. An oversized—27-ounce—goblet serves wine, Bloody Marys, gin and tonic, or punch with style.

To keep glassware sparkling clean, rinse in soda

water after washing to remove soap film. Beer, particularly, will have a better head and flavor if you do this.

If you are using plastic barware, go for stemless tumblers in clear silver. Get stable, well-made style. After-dinner liqueurs are best served in small glasses.

Measure for Pleasure

1 bottle of wine = about 6 glasses

1 fifth of liquor = about 15 drinks

1 quart of alcoholic punch = about 10 servings (4 ounces a glass)

1 dash = 6 drops

3 teaspoons = ½ ounce

1 jigger = 1½ ounces

1 oversized jigger = 2 ounces

1 fifth bottle = 25.6 ounces

For a twenty-five-guest cocktail party, you'll need approximately:

15 pounds of ice for drinks

2 quarts vodka

1 quart gin

2 quarts Scotch

2 quarts bourbon/sour mash

1 fifth dry vermouth

2 bottles light, special wines—sherry, Lillet, or Dubonnet

6 bottles white wine

16 bottles soda, tonic, ginger ale, diet soda

15 to 20 pounds ice in large tub to hold chilled wine and soda

Rule of thumb:

3 drinks per person at cocktail party.

2 drinks per person before dinner.

3 glasses of wine per person at dinner.

2 after-dinner cocktails per person.

BAR MENUS FOR ONE-DRINK PARTIES

We all know about the kinds of drinks that are served at standard parties. Now, there's nothing wrong with a glass of Scotch or a gin and tonic. But if you want to make your bar menus more interesting—and less expensive—consider the following:

WINE BAR

Wine is an exciting alternative to common mixed drinks. It can be served with appetizers, before dinner, at a cocktail party, throughout a meal, and after dinner, too. There is an awesome array of wines—sweet, dry, dark or pale, expensive or cheap. All this means you need some help when you select a good wine. You don't have to be an expert yourself, but you do need to be able to tell the difference between a good wine and a bad one.

• Find a good wine store. It should have a wide variety of domestic and imported wines. A supply of good-quality, inexpensive wines indicates the management knows enough to go for quality, not just price and label. Ask for recommendations.

• Don't serve a wine you have never tasted unless it is a special vintage that you are "sure" of. If you are buying jug wines, California labels, or discount European wines, get an extra bottle. Taste it

[151]

yourself; don't let your guests be guinea pigs!

• Choose wines that complement the flavor of the food you are serving. For a wine-cocktail party, you may want to offer a selection of white and red wines:

—with fish, shellfish, or pork; pasta with cream or cheese sauce— white wine or chilled Beaujolais

—with soups—sweeter wines such as dry sherry or sauterne

—with red meats, pâté, lamb, game, pasta with meat or red sauce—red wine

—with poultry, fowl, and veal—red or white

—with cheese—red wine, port, sherry

—with dessert—sherry, champagne

—with coffee—port (or cognac and liqueurs)

—champagne can, of course, be served with anything!

• Generally speaking, white wines are served chilled, while reds are best at room temperature. Uncork red wines to let them "breathe" thirty minutes before serving. Champagne

should be chilled in ice, not in the refrigerator, if possible.

Presentation

• *Decanting wine.* This is a good technique for self-service bars. Always decant jug wines. You can't expect guests to heft those bottles! Red wines can easily be decanted because they are served at room tempera-

ture. If you decant white wines, place carafe or pitcher in a container of ice until you are ready to serve.

At the dinner table, you may choose to give each guest his own mini carafe of wine rather than to place wine bottles on the table. This would create a very pretty, festive look.

• *Using wine baskets and coolers.* Wicker wine baskets were originally de-

signed to hold old red wines at an angle so that their sediment would remain undisturbed. Nowadays, these baskets are usually used for effect—but a nice one.

White wine and champagne can be kept in ice in a wine cooler. You may improvise your own cooler by using a galvanized pail, spray-painted black, silver, or red. When pouring wine that has been in ice, wrap a large white cloth napkin around the bottom and sides of the bottle.

• *Putting wine bottles on dinner table.* Every bottle that comes to the table should be dressed. Tie a cotton napkin around neck of each bottle; it catches drips and looks attractive. Stick a daisy into knot for extra pizazz.

WINE PLUS

These spritzers and punches are festive ways to stretch your liquor budget and still create a special party look.

White Wine +

Mix:

Half a glass of white wine and half of soda water. Serve by the glass. Garnish with lemon, lime, cucumber sticks, or kiwi.

Mix:

One bottle dry white wine + 2 bottles champagne + 3 thinly sliced oranges.

Mix:

Two bottles dry white wine + either peaches, apricots, pineapple, or strawberries (about 2 cups' worth) + 1 cup sweet sherry.

Red Wine +

Mix:

Two bottles red wine, 2 bottles soda, ½ cup brandy,

[153]

sliced oranges or peaches, 2 cups orange juice, 1 cup lemon juice.

Mix:

One bottle sparkling burgundy, 1 bottle club soda, ¼ cup rum, ¼ cup cognac; add lemon juice and sugar to taste.

Presentation

These wines and punches can be served from a large pitcher or punch bowl. If you do not have a traditional punch bowl, try using a large glass salad bowl, ice bucket, or oversized kitchen pot—wrapped in a large cotton napkin, tied in a big knot. If you want to rent a bowl, look in the yellow pages for catering services. You can also contact local restaurants, country clubs, or social clubs to see about renting one from them.

Hot wines for after dinner or fireside picnics:

Mix:

One quart red wine + 2

sticks of cinnamon, 1 teaspoon allspice, the peel of an orange and a lemon + sugar to taste (about a tablespoon). Heat in saucepan, serve with stick cinnamon in glass mugs.

Mix:

One bottle Chianti + honey; cinnamon and cloves to taste. Heat in saucepan, serve with sliced orange garnish in glass mugs.

BEER BAR

Although beer may be too filling to serve to your guests *before* dinner, it can be very tasty with hors d'oeuvres at a cocktail party or with dinner. With the availability of beers and ales from all over the world, you can now put together a beer bar that is unusual and pleasing to the eye and the taste buds.

• Chill beer slowly in refrigerator, never in freezer, to about 40°. Ales, dark beers, stout, are served warmer. Some people drink them at

room temperature.

• Frosted, chilled glasses or mugs compliment beer's flavor. To maintain a frost, remove glasses from freezer and place upside down on ice-filled tray.

• True beer fanatics feel the "head" of a poured beer should equal about one-fourth the glass or mug.

Presentation

If you give a beer-bar cocktail party, there are some easy ways to make it a stylish affair.

• Buy a wide variety of beers—Japanese, Mexican, German, Chinese, Danish, Irish, and so on. Keep each nationality separate.

• Divide bar into distinct areas so that each type of beer has its own territory.

• Make table decorations appropriate to each nationality. For example, place bottles of German beer on a tray. Create a background with an old beer stein filled with daisies.

- Do not open bottles ahead of time. Have lots of bottle openers on the bar.
- Place a large wastepaper basket next to the glasses and mugs so that bottles can be disposed of immediately. Empty as often as necessary.
- Choose foods that represent the same variety of countries as the beer: guacamole, sausages, spareribs.

PUNCHES FOR BUNCHES

If you are throwing a big party, there is nothing so easy, economical, or pretty as serving a wonderful punch. It doesn't have to be a sweet, fruit-filled concoction. The recipes below are simple and elegant.

- Use fresh fruit juice whenever possible. If you use frozen, get unsweetened.
- Add carbonated liquids—ginger ale, soda, champagne—just before serving so they don't go flat.
- Use ice molds for cooling; cubes will melt and dilute a punch, particularly if it is sitting out in a punch bowl for a long period of time.
- Use fresh or canned fruits as subtle touches for color and flavor.

Decorative Ice Molds

To keep a punch cold without diluting it, and to dress it up without making it look as if it has launched a flotilla of fruit, you can create ice molds.

Use any decorative metal mold (a Bundt pan, Jell-O mold, or pâté form) or improvise by using a casserole with a weighted can in the center.

1. Draw cold tap water. Let it sit. Stir occasionally to get out all air bubbles.
2. Pour about 1½ inches of water in mold.
3. Set in freezer until almost solid—but with a slight slushiness.
4. Arrange slices of strawberries, lemon, oranges, kiwi, or almost any fruit into a pretty pattern. Push them gently into the slush.
5. Pour very cold tap water over layer of fruit so it is well covered.
6. Repeat process if mold is deep enough.
7. Unmold by running warm water over

metal. Don't get it onto ice!
8. Place mold back in freezer until ready to put into punch.

Note: Decorative ice molds can also be used for hors d'oeuvres. Freeze shells, strands of ivy leaves, daisies, or sparkly glitter in ice. Use to chill seafood, fresh vegetables, or salads.

Decorative Ice Cubes

For punch served from a pitcher, make fruit-filled ice cubes. Follow the same process as for ice molds.

Some people like to freeze juices: orange or pineapple for addition to gin or vodka drinks, tomato juice for Bloody Marys, or lime or lemon juice for sours.

WINE PUNCHES

Wine Plus on page 153 introduced the idea of wine punches and spritzers. A wide variety of possibilities exist, including champagne and brandy mixtures.

SPARKLING WHITE WINES OR CHAMPAGNES

There are many fine "champagnes" that don't actually come from that magic plot of French soil. Blanc de Blancs from France, as well as Spanish, Italian, and American bubbly, can be very tasty, and definitely more affordable than their French counterparts. If you are going to mix champagne with soda and other flavors anyway, skip the pricy stuff and go for the good-tasting but moderately priced labels.

Pink Carnation—for 20

5 bottles sparkling wine
3 bottles white German wine
1 bottle claret
2 quarts of strawberries sprinkled with sugar—if you like

Sugar berries and soak in white wine in refrigerator. When ready to serve, put berries and wine into bowl and add remaining, well-chilled ingredients. Add ice mold. Serve only one berry in each glass when serving.

The Sweet with the Bitter—for 6 to 8

3 bottles sparkling white wine
1 cup brandy
sugar and bitters

Put sugar and bitters in bowl. Cover with brandy. Add ice mold and champagne immediately before serving.

Smoothie—for 6 to 8

Combine in blender 1 quart of strawberries, lemons, or boysenberries, or canned fruits such as pears, ap-

ricots, or peaches, with ½ to 1 cup cognac or naturally flavored brandy. Pour mixture over ice mold in punch bowl. Add 3 bottles bubbly and serve.

HARD PUNCHES

Make these drinks by the pitcherful! Garnish the glasses attractively. Mix up batches; keep in refrigerator to refill pitchers as needed.

Vodka Bog—for 15 to 20

1 bottle vodka
2 quarts cranberry juice
4 ounces cranberry liqueur
frozen concentrated orange juice (1 can)
soda to taste and sparkle

Chill with ice mold in punch bowl or on the rocks in individual glasses. Garnish with a thin slice of orange.

Rum Punch—for 20

2 fifths dark rum
1 fifth brandy
2½ to 3 cups fresh lemon juice

[157]

1 cup sugar
½ cup fruit-flavored brandy
32 ounces water

Combine ingredients. Let sit for 2 hours. Put ice in individual glasses, and ice mold into punch, just before serving.

Bloody Mary—for 6

48 ounces tomato juice
¼ cup dashes Worcestershire
10 dashes Tabasco
3 teaspoons horseradish
juice of 1½ lemons
9 jiggers vodka/tequila/ aquavit
pepper/celery salt, to taste
Garnish with stalk celery and lime.

Margarita—for 6

5 jiggers tequila
½ jigger triple-sec
2 ounces lime juice

Serve straight up or on the rocks. Garnish with a rim of salt on each glass.

Daiquiri—for 6

6 jiggers rum
½ ounce sugar syrup
1½ ounces lime juice

Serve with crushed ice. Garnish with a slice of lime.

AFTER-DINNER DRINKS

Once again, we all know about the snifter of brandy or the small glass of Cointreau. Each is an effective, elegant closing to a meal. But if you are having an after-dinner party and want the drinks to make an impact, you may like the coffee combos suggested below.

For a small gathering or an assembly-line service for a large, late-night party:

Coffee:

Brew two types of coffee— American and espresso. You can make espresso in any filter pot. Simply buy espresso dark roast beans, or a can of Medaglia d'Oro coffee.

Additions to American Coffee:

Kalhúa, Strega, Anisette, Tia Maria, Cognac, Cointreau, Irish Whiskey
Whipped cream
Shaved chocolate
Cinnamon—stick or powder
Orange/lemon peel
Set out a buffet with various liqueurs, coffee, whipped cream, chocolate, and citrus peel. Let guests make their own concoctions.

Espresso Plus:

Serve with a twist of lemon. For a little more jazz, add hot cream, cinnamon, and a dash of cognac.

Frozen Coffee:

Brew espresso (or regular) coffee. Pour into pie plate or ice cube tray. Flavor with dash of cinnamon, if desired. Freeze until almost solid. You should be able to mix it up into a slush that can be spooned into a tall goblet. Top with whipped cream. Garnish with grated bittersweet chocolate. Eat with a spoon.

Flambé Fire!—for 8

In a punch bowl, combine peel of 1 orange and 1 lemon, 3 cinnamon sticks,

5 teaspoons of sugar, and 1 cup hot (but not boiling!) brandy. Pour over fruit.

Fill large spoon with warm brandy. Hold just above ingredients. *Ignite* brandy in spoon; lower into brandy covering fruit. Do this in a darkened, guest-filled room for maximum drama. Add 4 to 6 cups of coffee. Top with ¼ cup of Cointreau.

COOKING WITH WINE AND LIQUOR

A chapter on liquor cannot end without a mention of the extraordinary contribution it can make to the flavor and specialness of food. From main dishes to dessert, every kind of food, every course in a meal, can be enhanced by the use of wine, liquor, or liqueurs.

Of course, you'll need to consult individual recipes for more details, but these guidelines and suggestions should help you get started. Cooking with wine and liquor is one of the easiest Jazz-It-Up touches you can use.

• A light touch is the rule. Always add a little at a time. Let it cook. Taste and then adjust if needed.
• Cooking removes the alcoholic content of liquor.
• As a general rule, add the kind of wine to any food you would drink it with. White wine with fish dishes, for example, or red in beef stew.
• Sweet wines, Dubonnet, Lillet, sherry, add flavor to most meat and poultry dishes. Cheese spreads (Roquefort, cheddar, gourmandise) are another way to use these wines. Add two tablespoons to each cup of cheese spread.
• Desserts are also a prime territory for the flavoring benefits of liquors and wines. Try them on fresh and canned fruit, ice cream, pound and sponge cakes, in puddings and baked cobblers.

"Celebrate your successes!"

CHAPTER •12•

IT'S PARTY TIME!

You've been my guests throughout this book. And I must say I've had fun. I hope you did, too.

Now it's time for you to assemble some guests of your own. I know you can do it. Although there *is* a lot to giving a successful party, you've seen that it is well within your grasp. You have style, and no matter what your time or budget, there are many ways to entertain successfully.

When you close this book, don't close your mind to the new and exciting entertaining ideas we've explored. Jump in. Get your feet wet. It's okay to start small if you're timid. Does it still seem a little audacious to turn your bed into a dining table? Well, have four close friends over and give it a try. Once you've done it in a "safe" way, you'll gain confidence.

Are you reluctant to try out the Rockery Table setting? Give it a test run for your family or one friend. Experiment a little before you go public. Remember to see the world "as if" it were a stage for your visions of entertaining. Keep your imagination alive. Bring one branch or flower into the house. Play with it. Try putting it in many different vases and locations. Have fun.

If there is one thing I hope I have been able to communicate to you throughout this book, it is that successful entertaining is a sure way to improve the quality of your life. It increases your self-confidence, enhances the beauty of your home and surrounds you with affection and friendship. Come on, reach out and enjoy life!

Marjorie Reed delights in entertaining and does it so imaginatively that she was cited in **The Bloomingdale's Book of Entertaining** as one of today's most creative hostesses. As assistant to famed couturier Mainboucher for three years, Directress of Arnold Scaasi for eight years, and more recently co-hostess of her own television program, "The Evening Show," Ms. Reed is equally at home in the world of fashion and entertaining.

Kalia Lulow is the co-author of **Vision Training** (with Dr. Edward Friedman) and **How to Clear Up Your Skin in 30 Days** (with Dr. Jonathan Zizmor); **Helena Rubenstein's Book of The Sun**, for which she was also the associate editor and illustrator; **Super Flyer: The Air Travelers Handbook** (with Laura Torbet); and is the collaborator on **How to Fight Fair with Your Kids and Win**. She worked on story development for "3-2-1 Contact," for the Children's Television Workshop, as well as for several film documentaries. Her freelance writing includes feature articles for Hearst Publications and King Features.

Robert Penny was educated in fine arts at the University of North Carolina, Chapel Hill, and the School of Visual Arts in New York. His illustrations and designs have appeared in the Potpourri Press Cookbook series, and the soon to be published *Fancy Folds*, by Linda Hetzer. Mr. Penny is a regular contributor to **Good Housekeeping, Cosmopolitan, Brides,** and **New York** magazine. He lives and works in New York.